Bridge in the Fourth Dimension

Bridge in the Fourth Dimension

Further Adventures of the Hideous Hog

Victor Mollo

B T Batsford Ltd, London

First published 1974
First Batsford edition 1996
Reprinted 2001

ISBN 0 7134 8004 1
A CIP catalogue record for this book is available from the British Library.

Printed and bound in Great Britain by The Bath Press, Bath

Published by B T Batsford Ltd, 9 Blenheim Court,
Brewery Road, London N7 9NY

A member of the Chrysalis Group plc

Contents

Acknowledgments

Most of the material in these pages has appeared in *Bridge Magazine*, where the Griffins and the Unicorns were born more than ten years ago. I am grateful to Eric Milnes, the Editor, for permission to reproduce.

I am indebted to the many friends of the Hideous Hog and the Rueful Rabbit who have asked me to write a sequel to *Bridge in the Menagerie*.

Finally, I am under a considerable obligation to the Hog himself. I have defamed his character and he could undoubtedly obtain damages for the wrong I have done him. With characteristic magnanimity, and for other still more compelling reasons, he has undertaken not to sue me. I hope that the rest of the cast will show similar indulgence.

Author's Preface

As the lights go up in the Griffins Club and at the Unicorn, the points of the compass spring to life. With rich red blood coursing through their veins, North and South, East and West, don flesh and bones and race across the traditional diagram to a battlefield where men are men, seeking no mercy and showing none.

If bridge is the most fascinating of all games, it is because it is the least contrived and the most human, allowing each player full scope to show not only his cleverness and skill, but likewise his faults and frailties, and to enjoy his failures almost as much as his successes.

Can the player's vivid dreams come true in a book? To bring this about must be every author's purpose.

He sets out with a clear advantage. Leaving aside the prosaic deals which predominate at the card-table, he can conjure up coup after coup to dazzle and to bemuse as he passes on to the reader the secrets of bridge expertise.

There's a price to pay. The triumphs and disasters of the written page bring neither elation nor despair, for they are abstract and no one is deeply stirred by the fate of lifeless puppets around a paper diagram. The human element is missing and that is the fourth dimension which makes bridge real and vibrant, raising it in stature above all other pastimes.

Of course it is intellectually satisfying to study the mechanics of a squeeze by South against West, but it doesn't arouse the senses. How much more exciting to watch a duel between man and man, following the Hideous Hog as he strives to squeeze or smother his arch-enemy, Papa the Greek? Or to kibitz the Rueful Rabbit defeating a seemingly unbreakable contract by stumbling inadvertently on an inspired defence?

There are no fictitious characters in this book. The reader has met them all and will easily recognize their features beneath the allegorical guise.

He will soon identify Walter the Walrus, who counts rather than plays bridge and would sooner go down honourably with 30 points than bring home a dubious contract on flimsy values. He has often played with, and above all, listened to Karapet, the unluckiest player in the Western Hemisphere—and in the Eastern Hemisphere, too, of course. And who hasn't suffered from the pedantries of the Secretary Bird, always prone to invoke the letter of the law, even if it brings about his own undoing?

Just as the dramatis personae are drawn from real life, so are the situations in which they find themselves. If some of them seem contrived, it is only because fact is stranger than fiction and bridge is often stranger than either.

'Life is real, life is earnest', and so is bridge. But need it ever be grim? And should it ever be dull? Of course not.

All humans are at times ridiculous, more often perhaps than they suspect. Hence the frequent touches of the burlesque in these pages. If the players were never comic, bridge itself would not be what it is—a magic mirror reflecting all the varied facets of human nature. Through this fourth dimensional mirror I invite the reader to follow the exploits of the Griffins and the Unicorns and to share fully their experiences. And now it only remains to switch on the lights.

1. Bridge with the Unicorns

'The bane of duplicate,' declared the Hideous Hog, 'is its soul-destroying predictability. It's morbid. It's melancholy. And it makes for mediocrity. When a man knows that someone in the other room holds the same cards as he does, what incentive has he to make twice two come to five? Why should he bother when the other fellow may not even get the addition up to four?'

We were dining at the Unicorn, where we Griffins seek refuge during the first fortnight in August while the staff at our own club take their annual holiday.

Every year we see new faces—and old faces, renovated by time, and almost as good as new. We come up against new conventions, new hoary anecdotes, new clichés, and the Hog finds new victims to dazzle, to bemuse and to enrich him—though that, as he would say himself, is purely incidental.

The first of August was particularly hot with the thermometer rising to twenty-four degrees Centigrade. It was hotter still Fahrenheit. Having disposed of an iced Cantaloup, the Hog returned to one of his favourite subjects—the iniquities of duplicate.

'At rubber bridge', he was saying, 'you win only by playing well. At duplicate it is enough not to play badly. The winners are simply those who chuck least. What a bleak and dreary way of life! Can you imagine Shakespeare or Michelangelo or Beethoven being satisfied with not making mistakes? Would Botticelli have given us the Divina Comedia just by not chucking?'

None of us seemed to know, but as H.H. was about to continue he was stopped short by a scathing snake-like noise. It came from the sole occupant of the next table, a man in his late fifties mounted on long, thin legs with a bird-like face and round bright eyes flashing from behind a pair of rimless glasses. Behind the ears of his small, globe-shaped head, projecting at right angles,

were tufts of wild white hair. 'Botticelli!' he hissed. 'Ignoramus!'
A strong current of mutual dislike quickly passed between the
Hog and the long, thin man.

'Who's that Secretary Bird?' asked H.H. scornfully, addressing
Peregrine the Penguin, the Unicorn's Senior Kibitzer, who was
our host. Then, interrupting the Penguin smartly before he could
begin, the Hog resumed his disquisition:

'The true significance of bridge is that it faithfully mirrors life
itself. The strong reap the reward of their strength. The weak are
justly punished for their weakness and the winners rightly enjoy
the esteem of their fellowmen,' he inclined his head modestly,
'which is as it should be. Not only is justice done, but it can be
seen to be done.

'But,' declared the Hog with solemnity, looking like a pink,
sleek edition of some ancient prophet, 'duplicate sets at naught
Nature's moral code. Butcher a hundred contracts. Massacre a
hundred partners. Commit *felo de se*. Misbid, misplay, misdeal.
It will not make a pennyworth of difference. You can sin with
impunity for you play for matchpoints and there is no distinction
between right and wrong. And that is why I say that playing
bridge not for money is immoral. It is a perversion, for Nature
had not intended it that way.'

As we made our way to the card room, the Hog fired a final
salvo:

'Duplicate is all very well for the weak, unlucky players, who
cannot expect much out of life anyway. They can take pride in
being beaten by masters. The greater the master, the greater the
honour. But who is going to look after the masters? Or do you
really think that doing execution should be its own reward?

'It's high time', concluded the Hog, glancing round for a table,
'that someone spoke up for the strong against the weak. The
underdogs have had it all their own way far too long.'

From a corner table, reverberating through the room, came a
penetrating, resonant voice, proclaiming proudly: 'I had sixteen.'
The voice belonged to a large ginger Walrus moustache behind
which sat a fat man with pale blue watery eyes.

Looking round the room, we could see only one Griffin—Colin,
a facetious young man, shaped rather like a corgi, who had only
recently come down from Oxbridge. He was partnering the

Walrus moustache, and one could tell at a glance that they did not love each other deeply, if at all.

We drifted towards their table and before long we heard the Walrus announce:

'What could *I* do? I had only thirteen!'

Apparently, a cold grand slam had just been played in a part-score. The Walrus had opened 1 ◊, which the Corgi had raised to 2 ◊ and there it stopped.

Their two hands were:

W.W.		*C.C.*
♠ —	N	♠ 7 6 4 2
♡ A J 4 3	W E	♡ K Q 5
◊ A 9 8 7 6 5 2	S	◊ K 10 4 3
♣ A 4		♣ 5 3

'A bare thirteen,' repeated the Walrus.

'Well played Walter,' said the Corgi when the thirteenth trick had been safely gathered, 'a nice, safe contract and the hundred above the line is just as good as having honours. What's more, with forty below, we need only another two grand slams like this one to give us game.'

With a grunt of pleasurable anticipation, the Hog seated himself by the Walrus. If there was going to be any sarcasm, bitterness and ill-feeling, that was definitely the table for him.

It was now Game All and 40 to North-South. West dealt and opened 1 ♠. This was the brief, but telling auction.

West	North C.C.	East	South W.W.
1 ♠	Pass	2 ♡	2 NT
Dble	ALL PASS		

West opened the ♠ 6.

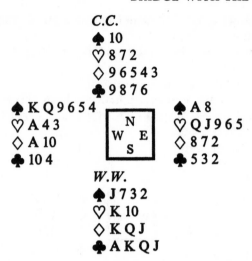

C.C.
♠ 10
♡ 8 7 2
♢ 9 6 5 4 3
♣ 9 8 7 6

♠ K Q 9 6 5 4   ♠ A 8
♡ A 4 3   ♡ Q J 9 6 5
♢ A 10   ♢ 8 7 2
♣ 10 4   ♣ 5 3 2

W.W.
♠ J 7 3 2
♡ K 10
♢ K Q J
♣ A K Q J

East went up with the ♠ A and returned the ♠ 8 on which the Walrus played the ♠ 3. Still on play, East switched to the ♡ Q.

Suppressing a cry of anguish, the Walrus covered with his king and lost the trick to West's ace. Four spades followed, declarer shedding a diamond honour and a club. Then came a heart and the Walrus, puffing indignantly, had to find three more discards. When East's last heart, the five, settled on the table, the position was:

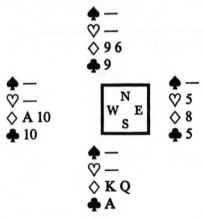

♠ —
♡ —
♢ 9 6
♣ 9

♠ —   ♠ —
♡ —   ♡ 5
♢ A 10   ♢ 8
♣ 10   ♣ 5

♠ —
♡ —
♢ K Q
♣ A

After trying each card in mid-air and muttering dark imprecations, the Walrus finally parted with the ♦ Q. It made no difference, of course, for West discarded after him and the defence was bound to win all thirteen tricks, inflicting a penalty of 2300.

'I had twenty-one-and-a-half points!' cried the Walrus indignantly, 'twenty in top cards, one point for distribution and half a point for the ten of hearts. Twenty-one and . . .'.

'Isn't something wrong?' broke in the Corgi softly. 'When you went down 1100 in 3 ♠ with me just now it was because you had 18½ points. Now with only three more you go down an extra 1200. Can it be that the point count is not mathematically foolproof? And how few points must you have to escape catastrophe altogether?'

Walter the Walrus was too shattered to respond to sarcasm. In an incredulous voice he kept saying: 'I had twenty-one. . . .'

The Hog's Debut

The Hog's first partner at the Unicorn was Colin, the facetious Corgi-shaped young man. They soon made a game. The Walrus, sitting West, dealt and opened 1 ♣. The Corgi doubled and East, a colourless Unicorn whose name even the Penguin couldn't remember, passed.

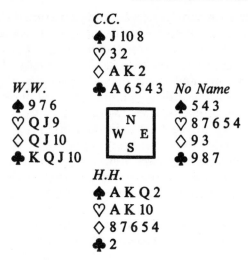

C.C.
♠ J 10 8
♡ 3 2
◇ A K 2
♣ A 6 5 4 3

W.W.
♠ 9 7 6
♡ Q J 9
◇ Q J 10
♣ K Q J 10

No Name
♠ 5 4 3
♡ 8 7 6 5 4
◇ 9 3
♣ 9 8 7

H.H.
♠ A K Q 2
♡ A K 10
◇ 8 7 6 5 4
♣ 2

This was the auction:

West	North	East	South
W.W.	Corgi	No Name	H.H.
1 ♣	Dble	Pass	2 ♣
Pass	2 NT	Pass	3 ♠
Pass	3 NT	Pass	4 ◇
Pass	4 ♠	Pass	5 ♡
Pass	6 ♣	Pass	6 ♡
Pass	7 ♠	Pass	Pass
Dble	ALL PASS		

The Corgi admitted readily enough, when challenged by a Kibitzer, that his take-out double was shaded, to say the least, but having signed off three times he felt justified in accepting a pressing invitation.

'And anyway,' he added with a sly look at the Walrus, 'reputations should be worth something, er . . . *his* and *hers*, if you see what I mean.'

The Walrus, who had doubled in a voice of thunder, opened the ♣ K.

'Thank you partner,' said H.H. sweetly. The cordial note in his voice was a measure of the disgust inspired by the sight of dummy.

It would have been poor tactics to encourage opponents by betray-
ing signs of his disappointment. From every pore he exuded
confidence and *bonhomie*.

But meanwhile, the problem remained. Was there any way of
making thirteen tricks?

The hand could be played pretty well double dummy for his
opening bid marked the Walrus with every missing honour. But
was that going to be much help?

I saw Peregrine the Penguin shake his head. Two Unicorns,
who were waiting to cut in, shrugged their shoulders and walked
away dejectedly.

After winning the first trick with dummy's ace, the Hog played
a club and ruffed it in his hand with the queen. Then came a
diamond to the table and another club ruffed high, followed by a
second diamond and a third club ruff, this time with the ace of
trumps.

The Hideous Hog now led the ♠ 2 and successfully finessed the
♠ 8, leaving this position:

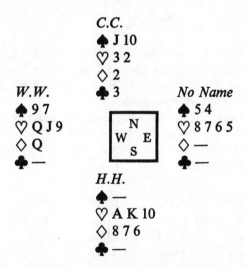

After drawing trumps, the Hog led the ♣ 2, throwing on it his
last diamond and retaining the ♡ A K 10. The Walrus was
inexorably squeezed in the red suits. After much puffing he let go
his ♡ 9 and ten seconds later it was all over.

B

'I . . .' he began.

'You had twelve points and two tens. I'll say it for you,' broke in Colin quickly.

The Secretary Bird Cuts In

I went across the room to make up another table and for an hour or so I lost track of the Hog, though I could still hear the Walrus announcing his point count in tones that were sometimes plaintive, sometimes angry, and often surprised.

Then the Secretary Bird joined the Hog's table. Even at a distance I could feel the exchange of snarl and hiss as he took his seat.

When I cut out and went over to watch, I found H.H. sitting with:

♠ K 5 4 3 2
♡ 6
◇ A 6 5 4 3
♣ A K

As I sat down, he was saying: 'Double.' His partner, the Unicorn without a name, had opened 1 ♣ and the Secretary Bird (East) had called 1 NT. Walter the Walrus, sitting West, bid 2 ♡ and this was followed by two passes.

The Hog looked across at his partner, noted the awkward way in which he fumbled with his cards, and with a look of ill-concealed dislike, applied the classical Rabbit treatment: 3 NT. This was the sequence:

North	East	South	West
No Name	S.B.	H.H.	W.W.
1 ♣	1 NT	Dble	2 ♡
Pass	Pass	3 NT	

I could read his thoughts. Yes, 4 ♠ or 5 ◇ might prove to be a better contract than 3 NT. But with so dim-witted a creature opposite how could one hope to find out? Besides, there was always the risk that unless one acted quickly the wrong man would play the hand.

The Walrus led the ♡ 3 and the nameless Unicorn put down dummy.

No Name
♠ Q 6
♡ A K 5 4
◊ Q 2
♣ J 10 9 8 7

```
      N
  W       E
      S
```

H.H.
♠ K 5 4 3 2
♡ 6
◊ A 6 5 4 3
♣ A K

'Bit of a misfit,' murmured a kibitzer.

'What a contract!' observed another.

Even without the heart lead, the club suit looked pretty dead, for on the bidding, neither of dummy's queens was likely to provide an entry and declarer would need two to set up the clubs and enjoy them.

The Hog played low from dummy to the opening heart lead and the Secretary Bird, winning with the knave, continued with the queen. H.H. threw on it his ♣ K, won the trick in dummy with the ♡ K and followed with the ♡ A on which he discarded from his hand the ♣ A. Next came the ♣ J. The Secretary Bird won it with the ♣ Q and returned another. He had clearly no intention of leading up to dummy's queens.

The Hog proceeded to cash his clubs, which broke 4–2. On the last one the Secretary Bird threw the ◊ 10 suggesting that his pattern was 3–3–3–4. There was still a hope—that his spade holding was A J 10. Then he could be thrown in to lead a diamond away from the king. I peered into the other hands. This was the complete deal:

No Name
♠ Q 6
♡ A K 5 4
◇ Q 2
♣ J 10 9 8 7

W.W.
♠ 10 8 7
♡ 10 8 7 3 2
◇ 9 8 7
♣ 3 2

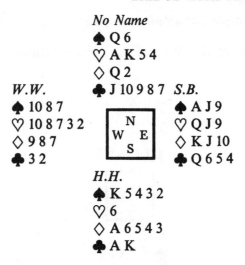

S.B.
♠ A J 9
♡ Q J 9
◇ K J 10
♣ Q 6 5 4

H.H.
♠ K 5 4 3 2
♡ 6
◇ A 6 5 4 3
♣ A K

Having finished with the clubs, H.H. made a rather weird looking play of the low spade away from dummy's queen. The Secretary Bird followed with the nine and the Hog, winning with the king, played back another spade. There was now no way of escape for S.B. for he only had the ♠ A J and the ◇ K J left.

'Very lucky,' he hissed. 'I had every card that mattered and could not move.'

'Ha!' jeered the Hog.

'Are you suggesting,' asked S.B., his spectacles gleaming dangerously, 'that I could have broken the contract?'

'No. *You* couldn't,' replied H.H. 'Anyone else, however, might have put up the ♠ J instead of the nine.'

The Secretary Bird tried to think of a crushing retort, but nothing suitably venomous came to him on the spur of the moment.

The Hog did not mind. He was engaged in his favourite pastime, adding up the score.

2. The Rabbit Takes Charge

'Am I as bad as you think I am?' The question was put to me by the Rueful Rabbit as he toyed with the heart of an artichoke over lunch at the Unicorn. Before I could form a suitably evasive reply, he went on:

'They all think me crazy, you know, to play at high stakes with the Hideous Hog or even with Papa, for that matter. Don't they realize that it's perfectly couth to lose to champions. It's taking a beating from palookas that's so humiliating. Of course,' went on the Rabbit, 'it costs more to be thrashed by a first-class man. But one should not quibble, when it comes to paying for one's pleasure, and, when all is said and done, there's such a thing as self-respect. If not, the least one can do is to pretend there is. Think, too, of the thrill of putting it across the experts! You can't get the better of them at golf or tennis or chess, no matter how much you pay. But it happens at bridge. Sometimes, the champions are too good or too clever and beat themselves. Sometimes you hold all the cards, which makes them very cross indeed. And sometimes, if you get into the swing of it, you can manage to be lucky. That's the part I like best.

'Of course,' confided the Rabbit, sipping his Rosé d'Anjou, 'it's all a matter of degree. If I were clueless, like that poor Walrus or the Secretary Bird—Professor of something, isn't he?—I wouldn't play at all. Looking ridiculous in public is undignified. But then, I am sure, that you don't put me in that class?'

'A most agreeable wine,' I replied, 'so light and refreshing. To follow, with your strawberries, I recommend a glass of the Corton '64.'

Leaving the Rabbit to a bowl of Royal Sovereigns, I made hastily for the door. As I went through, I cannoned into Walter the Walrus.

'Nice to have you Griffins here while your own club is being done up or something,' he boomed. Then, dropping his voice to a confidential bellow, he went on: 'I suppose the standard at the Griffins is pretty low. Even so, how can that chap you were lunching with, that Rabbit, manage to survive? Millionaire, I suppose . . . game must cost him a fortune . . . can't tell one card from another . . . can't even sort them out . . . amazing. Do you know what he did to me yesterday?'

'Yes, I heard about it,' I lied hopefully. But it didn't help. He told me just the same. He started on another hand, but at last fortune smiled and the steward came in looking for someone who had booked a long-distance call to Tiverton, Tomsk or maybe it was Tegucigulpa. I forget now which it was, but I confessed at once that I was the caller and quickly darted round a corner, past the telephone booths and into the card-room. The Secretary Bird was the sole tenant. I tried to look inconspicuous, but I was spotted at once. A pair of long, thin wiry legs approached me. Looking up I could see two wild tufts of hair growing at right angles to the ears. Between them was a pair of bright round eyes sending out a brilliant dazzle from somewhere in outer space.

'You are a student of human nature,' was his opening gambit, 'tell me, then, why is it that it happens at bridge? People who croak like frogs don't insist on singing opera, at least not all the time. The lame do not take to sprinting. Yet men with anti-card sense developed to the highest pitch, play bridge every day. Take your Rabbit or our Walrus. Surely, each in turn must know that but for the other he would be the worst player in the world. Why, then, don't they stick to marbles or noughts and crosses? Why bridge? I must tell you a hand. . . .'

I was saved in the nick of time by an influx of players from the dining-room.

'Remind me to tell you about the hand later,' hissed the Secretary Bird as he cut an ace to find himself opposite the Hideous Hog. Neither made any attempt to hide his dislike of the other. The ◊ 2 and the ♣ 3 brought together Walter the Walrus and the Rueful Rabbit. They looked at each other with well-founded apprehension.

In pleasurable anticipation, I sat down by the side of the Rabbit. I was not going to miss this spectacle of the blind leading the blind.

'You Griffins, I know, all like the weak no trump,' intoned the Walrus, 'very well, we'll. . . .'

'No, no,' broke in the Rabbit nervously, 'you Unicorns prefer the strong no trump. I'll play your way. . . .'

'No, yours, really. . . .'

'I . . . well . . . er . . . we. . . .'

This was the first hand of the afternoon.

Dealer North: Love All

<pre>
                        W.W.
                      ♠ J 8 6 2
                      ♡ Q 4 3 2
                      ◇ A K Q
        S.B.   ♣ A 10   H.H.
      ♠ 10 9   ♠ Q 7 5 4
      ♡ J 10 9 8   ┌─────┐   ♡ 7 5
      ◇ J 7 6 5   │ N │   ◇ 4 3 2
      ♣ Q J 2   W │   │ E   ♣ 8 7 6 5
                      │ S │
                      └─────┘
                        R.R.
                      ♠ A K 3
                      ♡ A K 6
                      ◇ 10 9 8
                      ♣ K 9 4 3
</pre>

North	East	South	West
W.W.	H.H.	R.R.	S.B.
Pass	Pass	1 NT	Pass
4 NT	Pass	5 ♡	Pass
5 NT	Pass	6 ♠	Pass
6 NT	ALL PASS		

This sequence, and especially North's pass as dealer, may appear curious to the uninitiated. The Walrus, however, was in considerable difficulty. Falling in with the habits of a brittle partner, he was playing a weak no trump and a cruel Fate had dealt him a strong one. He had no biddable suit. What could he do but pass?

Thinking of the frailties of the Walrus, the Rabbit had espoused the strong no trump. Each, in turn, was anxious to protect the weaker brother. Blackwood explains the rest, for of course W.W. had to catch up somehow after his original pass, and, of course, R.R. responded conventionally, as always, to 4 NT.

S.B. opened the ♠ 10 to the knave, queen and king. The Rabbit led out enthusiastically his winners, the ◇ A K Q, the ♡ A K Q and the ♠ A. He even noticed the fall of the ♠ 9 and cashed the ♠ 8 with aplomb. The Secretary Bird, who had false-carded cunningly in following to the hearts, now let go the thirteenth diamond. The four-card end position was:

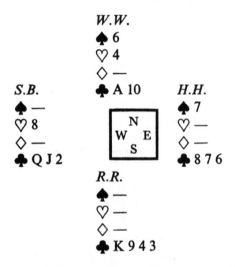

W.W.
♠ 6
♡ 4
◇ —
♣ A 10

S.B.
♠ —
♡ 8
◇ —
♣ Q J 2

H.H.
♠ 7
♡ —
◇ —
♣ 8 7 6

R.R.
♠ —
♡ —
◇ —
♣ K 9 4 3

The Rabbit checked his figures. After a final count, he found that he needed three more tricks and he proceeded to look for them in every direction.

Was the ♠ 6 good? Was that little heart? One could not always be certain about such things, but the percentage play, as the Rabbit explained later, favoured the spade. The six being better than the four there was a greater chance that it would turn out to be a master.

The Rabbit duly tried the ♠ 6. The Hog won it with the ♠ 7 and the S.B. was well and truly fixed. With a hiss he let go the ♣ 2. Seeing a club honour come up on the next trick, R.R. could hardly go wrong.

'I was hopelessly squeezed in hearts and clubs,' lamented S.B.

'True,' agreed H.H., 'but you should have given yourself a chance by throwing the ♣ Q on the last spade, keeping the two for the next trick. The Rabbit might have been tempted to win cheaply with the ten and in the process he would have locked himself in dummy. You failed to lead him into temptation. A mistake against any opponent. Against R.R., it's a sin.'

This was the next deal:

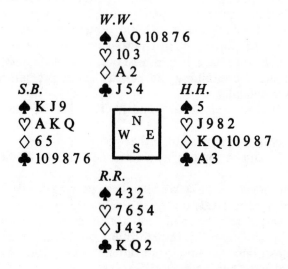

W.W.
♠ A Q 10 8 7 6
♡ 10 3
◇ A 2
♣ J 5 4

S.B.
♠ K J 9
♡ A K Q
◇ 6 5
♣ 10 9 8 7 6

H.H.
♠ 5
♡ J 9 8 2
◇ K Q 10 9 8 7
♣ A 3

R.R.
♠ 4 3 2
♡ 7 6 5 4
◇ J 4 3
♣ K Q 2

As usual, when he held dreary cards, R.R's attention wandered. He fidgeted. He played with his pencil. Surreptitiously he peeped at an evening paper which someone had left at a table by his side. In fact, the Rabbit was bored.

The auction was short and simple. The Hog opened proceedings with 1 ◇ and the Secretary Bird closed them with a direct jump to 3 NT.

W.W. opened the ♠ 8. He knew nothing of the eleven rule, of course, but he regarded it as unbecoming, if not downright immoral, not to lead the fourth highest of his longest suit.

Winning with the nine in his hand, S.B. led a diamond to dummy's king, then a heart back to his hand. At this point, he paused, hissed gently and meditated. All depended on those diamonds and either defender might have the ace or knave or both. Before leading the suit again to put it to the test, S.B. played off his top hearts, opening the way for dummy's ♡ J.

Tired of a contract which he could see no hope of breaking, the Rabbit was playing carelessly before his turn. Twice the Secretary Bird remonstrated, flicking cigarette ash irritably on the table as was his wont. When R.R. erred again, following to the third round of hearts before the Walrus could find a suitable discard, S.B. turned on him angrily: 'I have asked you repeatedly to wait your turn. Since you find it too much trouble, I am compelled to invoke the rules.' Looking every inch the Emeritus Professor of Bio-Sophistry, the Secretary Bird picked up the Laws on Contract Bridge, turned to page 31 and read out, with gusto, subsection (c) of section 57, prescribing the penalty for a premature lead or play by a defender.

The Walrus spluttered loudly. The Rabbit gurgled nervously.

'If I am right in presuming that you have no heart,' said S.B., sternly, 'I request you to play a diamond.' He was the boss and he knew it.

At this point, the Hog, who had been peering into W.W's cards, weighed in vehemently on the side of his opponents.

'Surely, partner,' he cried, 'you are not going to take advantage of this insignificant, this imperceptible peccadillo; a merest trifle. Be magnanimous. Show your innate generosity. Our friend's technical error has made no difference. . . .'

'A diamond. In accordance with the Laws, I specify the diamond suit,' insisted the Secretary Bird implacably.

The Walrus slammed his only remaining diamond, the ace, indignantly on the table. 'Sure you don't want my wallet as well?' he demanded, seething with rage.

'Respect for the Laws is the basis of civilized society,' rejoined S.B. serenely. But now the contract was doomed. With the ◊ A out of the way, the Rabbit's ◊ J became a certain entry and it was only a matter of seconds before a deadly spade was thrust through S.B's gizzard. Proudly invoking the Laws, he had encompassed his own destruction.

'Rarely have I seen a more brilliant piece of defence by declarer,' commented the Hog bitterly.

'Sorry, partner,' apologized the Rabbit, 'I will try to concen-

trate. It's the heat, you know. I have been trying to work it out
and I make it 147 centigrade—or is it celsius?'

The Rabbit was visibly rattled, and as so often happens, a slip
on one hand cast its shadows on the next. In contrite mood, R.R.
picked up:

♠ 5 3 2
♡ K 9 8 4 3 2
♢ A 2
♣ 9 4

That, at least, is how he sorted his cards. A closer inspection
would have revealed that he had five hearts only and the ♢ A 9 2.
In the heat of the moment, the ♢ 9 was inadvertently seconded to
the hearts.

West	North	East	South
S.B.	W.W.	H.H.	R.R.
1 ♢	Dble	Pass	2 ♡
4 ♢	5 ♡	Pass	6 ♡

With S.B. the dealer, this was the bidding:
The Secretary Bird opened the ♢ K. This was the full deal:

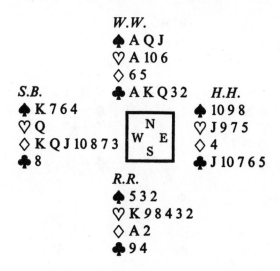

```
                    W.W.
                  ♠ A Q J
                  ♡ A 10 6
                  ♢ 6 5
  S.B.            ♣ A K Q 3 2      H.H.
  ♠ K 7 6 4         ┌───────┐     ♠ 10 9 8
  ♡ Q               │   N   │     ♡ J 9 7 5
  ♢ K Q J 10 8 7 3  │ W   E │     ♢ 4
  ♣ 8               │   S   │     ♣ J 10 7 6 5
                    └───────┘
                    R.R.
                  ♠ 5 3 2
                  ♡ K 9 8 4 3 2
                  ♢ A 2
                  ♣ 9 4
```

There was an inescapable diamond loser and a losing trump, maybe two.

Colin the Corgi, who was waiting to cut in, moved away. Peregrine the Penguin and two lesser kibitzers settled down comfortably and ordered long drinks.

The Rabbit won the opening lead with the ◇ A in his hand and led a trump to dummy's ace. Registering a jolt at the sight of S.B's queen, he set about the clubs, intent on getting rid of what he believed to be his only losing diamond.

There was another surprise for the Rabbit when the Walrus threw a small diamond on the second round of clubs. If he had no club, why didn't he ruff?

The Rabbit's lips twitched and his nostrils dilated with suspicion. Quickly, before either defender could change his mind, he led the ♣ Q, discarding the ◇ 2, his one and only—to the best of his knowledge and belief. Still S.B. did not ruff and all was well.

In his anxiety to dispose of that diamond, R.R. had neglected the spades. The issue could be postponed no longer. Squaring his round shoulders, the Rabbit came to hand by ruffing a club and successfully finessed against the ♠ K. Getting back with another club ruff he finessed again. Then he cashed the ♠ A and this was the three-card ending:

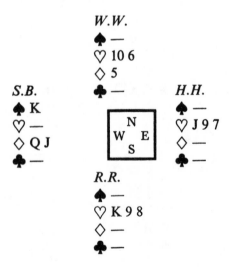

```
                    W.W.
                    ♠ —
                    ♡ 10 6
                    ◇ 5
        S.B.        ♣ —          H.H.
        ♠ K                      ♠ —
        ♡ —      ┌─────────┐     ♡ J 9 7
        ◇ Q J    │   N     │     ◇ —
        ♣ —      │ W   E   │     ♣ —
                 │   S     │
                 └─────────┘
                    R.R.
                    ♠ —
                    ♡ K 9 8
                    ◇ —
                    ♣ —
```

The Rabbit now led dummy's $\diamond$ 5. The Hog ruffed with the $\heartsuit$ 7 and R.R. 'over-ruffed'—with the $\diamond$ 9.

As the card touched the table, he blinked, blushed and burbled. Checking an involuntary attempt to retrieve it, he bowed his head in shame. Undoubtedly, that heart was a diamond. All because he was rattled by the previous hand, he had been careless on this one. It had happened to him before and would doubtless happen again. But what was the use of saying anything? People didn't understand these things.

The Hog glanced at him malevolently and damned that interfering guardian angel who turned all the Rabbit's misdemeanours to his advantage. Cursing under his breath, H.H. led the $\heartsuit$ 9. With a shrewd suspicion that S.B. was short of trumps, R.R. let the nine run up to dummy's ten, and a few seconds later it was all over. Somehow a diamond loser had evaporated and he lost only one trump.

'What happened?' asked R.R. in bewilderment.

3. Hog v Nemesis

The Hog sighed. Sipping dejectedly a Fernet Branca, the only drink to fit his bitter mood, he slumped back in his chair, a sitting target for good advice.

Partners and kibitzers alike had shown concern for a month or more at the Hog's uninterrupted run of bad luck. His daily winnings had dwindled into single figures and hardly a player in the cardroom was suffering worthwhile losses.

How could Nemesis be held at bay? How could the evil spell be broken? These were the questions which faced us, his closest friends and enemies as we gathered at the bar of the Griffins.

S.B., the Emeritus Professor, who had held the chair of Bio-Sophistry at Bingoville University, suggested consulting a witch doctor. He knew a distinguished practitioner who could cast or break any spell and accepted graciously francs, sterling or roubles; even dollars.

Walter the Walrus offered to present the Hog with a pocket computer which could calculate in minus two-fifths of a second how many points every player in the room had held during the preceding twelve months.

The Rueful Rabbit had little faith in witch doctors, computers or other forms of black magic, but he was acutely aware of Nemesis. Speaking from long and bitter experience he gave this advice: 'If she tries to fix you, jump in ahead and break up the pattern of her dark design. Anticipating the fall of the cards, she bewitches them. Anticipating your play of them, she cooks the distributions. Yet even Nemesis can't foresee the unforeseeable and if you set out to be irrational, you'll take her out of her stride. To break her spell, defy reason. Be absurd.'

'For money? My own money?' asked H.H. doubtfully.

'Try duplicate then', persisted R.R., 'with only match points at stake, what can the worst, the most stupid partner. . . .'

'Very well,' broke in the Hog, 'I invite you to play with me in the Unicorn's duplicate next Thursday.' And when the Rabbit had left us, he added: 'Picking that crazy Rabbit for partner! Nemesis will never guess that I could do a thing like that.'

That was how it all started.

22 Tricks on a View

The duplicate was nearing the halfway stage when I arrived at the Unicorn. Play had stopped for some reason and everyone was talking excitedly at once.

'What's holding them up?' I asked Peregrine the Penguin, Senior Kibitzer at the Unicorn.

'A case of misboarding, I believe,' explained the Penguin. 'According to the travelling score slip on board 11, East-West made three no trumps at one table while at another all thirteen tricks, likewise in no trumps, were made by North-South. Since that's manifestly impossible, they are trying to trace the error.'

At this point, the Tournament Director took the floor and announced: 'The results on board 11 have been checked and found to be correct as entered on the travelling score sheet. Please move for round 7.'

Gasps of incredulity all round and a burst of raucous laughter from the Hog greeted the announcement.

I heard the story of board 11 during the interval from Karapet, the Free Armenian, who was playing with Papa. It was common knowledge, of course, that in the fourteenth century the black witch of Ararat had put a curse on the Djoulikyans and the evil spell had never lost its potency.

Karapet showed us his hand which he had held as South on board 11.

Papa

♠ 6 2
♡ 5 4 3
♢ 6 5 4 2
♣ 8 5 4 2

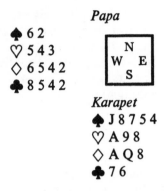

Karapet
♠ J 8 7 5 4
♡ A 9 8
♢ A Q 8
♣ 7 6

'East dealt and bid 3 NT,' began Karapet, 'the Acol type, you know, based on a solid minor. All passed. Maybe I should have opened one of my aces—not that it would have made much difference—but I did not fancy it. I led the ♠ 5. Reasonable?'

No one registered disapproval, so Karapet continued: 'Papa won with the king. Then he played the ace and a third spade, which declarer took with the queen. Six clubs followed bringing me down to four cards. Which should they be?'

'Any help from partner?' I asked.

'Judge for yourself,' replied the Armenian. After following once, Papa shed the ♡ 7, followed by the ♡ 2, then the ♢ 3, the ♢ 7 and ♢ 9.

Having exercised the Senior Kibitzer's traditional prerogative of ordering drinks, Peregrine the Penguin now joined in the discussion.

'You can't bare either ace,' he observed, 'otherwise declarer will throw you in with it to lead away from the other and that would cost two tricks.'

'True,' agreed Karapet, 'but note that if I keep the ♢ A Q and the ♡ A x, a diamond will still end-play me.'

'The contract will go one down, though,' said someone.

'Certainly,' said the Armenian, 'but that would be little better than a bottom for there was no doubt by this time that we could make two spades, if not three. For a decent score we had to get them two down at least.'

After a pause for cogitation, Karapet resumed. 'Partner could not have much, but he might just scrape together the ◇ J. If so, I could part with the ◇ Q and avoid the end-play.'

There was another pause, though this time no one pretended to cogitate.

'I threw the ◇ Q,' went on Karapet, 'keeping ace-small in both red suits. Declarer played the ◇ K, which I won with the ace, partner following with the ten. Since it was hardly likely, to judge by his discards, that he had the knave as well, my sole remaining hope was to find Papa with the ♡ K so. . . .'

'So in sheer desperation,' interposed the Penguin, 'you led the ace and your other heart.'

'But declarer turned up with the king, no doubt, and so made the contract,' put in someone unkindly.

'For all that, I played correctly,' declared the Armenian showing us all four hands. 'I was working for a good result, not for a tepid bottom as opposed to a cold one.'

This was the deal on board 11.

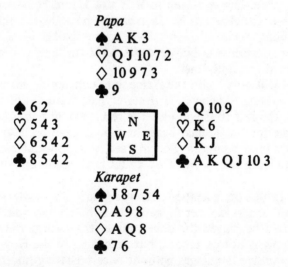

Papa
♠ A K 3
♡ Q J 10 7 2
◇ 10 9 7 3
♣ 9

♠ 6 2
♡ 5 4 3
◇ 6 5 4 2
♣ 8 5 4 2

♠ Q 10 9
♡ K 6
◇ K J
♣ A K Q J 10 3

Karapet
♠ J 8 7 5 4
♡ A 9 8
◇ A Q 8
♣ 7 6

We sympathized politely with the Armenian. The Penguin muttered something discreetly about Ararat.

'But what's this business about North-South making all thirteen tricks?' I asked. 'Was it the Rabbit who thought that he was playing Misère?'

C

'No, no,' Karapet assured me, 'the Rueful Rabbit, for once, did nothing calamitous. No one did. The odd thing, in fact, is that everyone behaved sensibly, though there was a difference of twenty-two tricks, as it were, between the results at our table and theirs—minus nine against plus thirteen—on the same cards.'

This, I was told, had been the sequence of events earlier in the evening when H.H. and R.R. met the Emeritus Professor of Bio-Sophistry. S.B., dealt and opened 1 ♣. After two passes, the Hog, sitting North, doubled protectively and S.B., feeling no doubt that he held plenty in hand, bid a tactical 1 NT. The Rabbit, in the South seat, doubled and much to the Professor's delight, 1 NT doubled became the final contract.

Like Karapet, R.R. opened the ♠ 5. The Hog went up with the ♠ A and returned the ♠ 3. The Professor knew well enough that the Hog might have the king behind the ace. Alternatively, he might have the knave. S.B. thought deeply before making the wrong guess. His ♠ 10 fell to R.R.s ♠ J, and he continued with the ♠ 4 to the Hog's ♠ K. Then came a heart switch, the Rabbit's ace killing declarer's king. Two more spades were succeeded by four more hearts before a diamond through the king-knave completed the holocaust.

'You will note,' said the Armenian, concluding his account of the slaughter, 'that even if declarer had started with three diamonds, the K J 10 if you like, the result would have been exactly the same for on the last heart he would have been squeezed inexorably in the minors. So, you see, not only did North-South make thirteen tricks, but they could have made one more, so to speak.'

The Professor, I heard later, was bearing his ordeal manfully, when an earnest kibitzer suggested to him that he would have done better had he played the queen rather than the ten at trick two. S.B's reply is not on record, but according to the Hog, he hissed fluently in five languages without once repeating himself.

Outbidding Destiny

After the interval, I joined Peregrine who was kibitzing the Hog. This was one of the early boards in the second half

Dealer West: Love All   *R.R.*

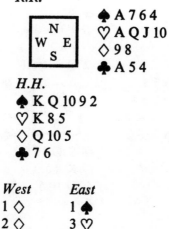

♠ A 7 6 4
♥ A Q J 10
♦ 9 8
♣ A 5 4

H.H.

♠ K Q 10 9 2
♥ K 8 5
♦ Q 10 5
♣ 7 6

West	East
1 ♦	1 ♠
2 ♦	3 ♥
3 NT	

The Rabbit opened the ♣ Q which declarer won in the closed hand with the ♣ K. A heart followed. Dummy's ten held the trick and declarer returned to his hand with the ♦ A to take the finesse once more. Again it succeeded, the Hog nonchalantly unguarding his ♥ K. A kibitzer swallowed the wrong way. Another nervously put out his cigarette in dummy's coffee cup. Unmoved, declarer led a diamond from the table to his king and for the third time he finessed the heart.

Winning with the bare king, the Hog took his ♦ Q and exited with a club. The contract could no longer be made.

'One down?' said dummy incredulously, scanning the travelling score sheet. 'At every other table the contract was made. Why should we alone get a minus?'

'Because you alone were pitted against me,' explained H.H. modestly. No one spoke. 'Very well,' he went on, 'since you are all so curious, I will let you into the secret of my double-dummy defence.' He jotted down the four hands.

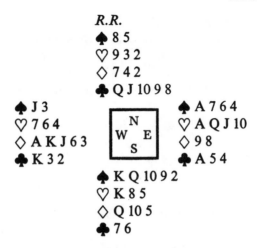

R.R.
♠ 8 5
♡ 9 3 2
◇ 7 4 2
♣ Q J 10 9 8

♠ J 3   ♠ A 7 6 4
♡ 7 6 4   ♡ A Q J 10
◇ A K J 6 3   ◇ 9 8
♣ K 3 2   ♣ A 5 4

♠ K Q 10 9 2
♡ K 8 5
◇ Q 10 5
♣ 7 6

'For the barest opening bid,' explained the Hideous Hog, 'declarer had to have five diamonds, if not six, headed by the A K J. Since the queen was on the right side, he was predestined to make his contract. How could I deflect destiny's course? Only by outbidding her, that is, by offering declarer something better. If I could persuade him to accept my guarantee for the heart finesse, he would not need the finesse in diamonds for he could get home with four hearts, two top diamonds, two top clubs and the ♠ A. And in hearts, mind you, the finesse alone would suffice. In diamonds, if he had five, he would need a 3–3 break as well.

'But of course,' went on the Hog, 'I could not admit to my ♡ K until declarer had used up the entries to his hand, all three of them, Baring the king looked risky to the kibitzers, but I had nothing to lose, really, for the contract was otherwise doomed to succeed. It was what I call a black eye-to-nothing coup. Either I don't lose or opponents get a black eye.'

1313 And all that

In the penultimate round H.H. and R.R. met Walter the Walrus and Timothy the Toucan. This was the deal:

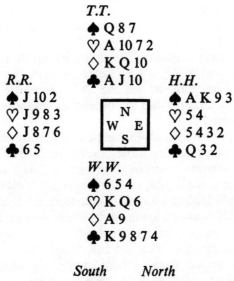

T.T.
♠ Q 8 7
♡ A 10 7 2
◇ K Q 10
♣ A J 10

R.R.
♠ J 10 2
♡ J 9 8 3
◇ J 8 7 6
♣ 6 5

H.H.
♠ A K 9 3
♡ 5 4
◇ 5 4 3 2
♣ Q 3 2

W.W.
♠ 6 5 4
♡ K Q 6
◇ A 9
♣ K 9 8 7 4

South	North
1 NT	3 NT

The Rabbit opened the ♠ J which held the trick. Then came the ♠ 10, covered by dummy's queen and won by the Hog with the king. The ♠ A followed, but cunningly concealing his ♠ 9, the Hog switched to the ◇ 3.

The Walrus tried the hearts, but when H.H. threw the ◇ 2 on the third round he was forced to look to the clubs for his ninth trick. Expecting R.R. to have the thirteenth spade, the Walrus took the club finesse against him.

'Surprise, surprise,' chanted the Hog as he pounced on the ♣ J with his queen and shot the ♠ 9 across the table.

For the last round I followed the board to Papa's table. A big hearty man with an orchid buttonhole was drinking champagne in the South seat. 'Who's that?' I asked the Penguin who had come with me.

'That's Jeremy Joybell,' said P.P. 'He's the export manager of our biggest syndicate of undertakers. The champagne is on expense account, of course. His partner is Lord Mortsbury, the head of the syndicate.'

Like the Walrus, J.J. became declarer at 3 NT and like the Rabbit, Karapet opened the ♠ J. It held the trick. Papa, who was

East, won the next two tricks with the king and ace. Like the Hog, the Greek cleverly concealed his last spade, playing at trick four the ◇ 2.

'Exactly the same sequence,' observed Peregrine the Penguin. J.J. tried the hearts. When they failed to break, he went into a short huddle. Emerging, he led the ♣ A, then the ♣ J. Papa played low and declarer ran it, raising an eyebrow when the Armenian followed suit.

The Greek threw his hands in the air in a gesture of despair. 'What made you take this unnatural finesse?' he cried, more in anger than in sorrow. You could not know that I had the last spade. How, then, could you, master player 1017, play so badly?'

Jeremy Joybell looked abashed. 'You took me in completely,' he confessed. 'Of course, I assumed that your partner had the last spade, so I placed you with three spades, two hearts and presumably four diamonds. You led the deuce and it seemed unlikely that you would choose a false card in this situation. That left you with four clubs, so that when the queen did not come down on the first round, it meant that you simply had to have it. Yes, I am afraid you bamboozled me badly with your defence.'

Peregrine turned to the Hog, who had finished his last set of boards and had come up to jeer at Papa.

'Is that why you carefully selected the ◇ 3 and then discarded the two,' asked the Penguin. 'So that Walter should have no clue to your distribution?'

'Bah!' That Walrus has no clue to anything anyway,' retorted H.H. 'But it's a matter of self-respect to play correctly even when one is alone.'

We could hear Papa calculating his bottoms at the next table.

'He was unlucky on that last board,' admitted the Hog grudgingly, 'for he played well up to a point, but he struck one of the few players in the room who was good enough to miscount his hand. Yes, for once, Papa was truly unlucky.'

'Unlucky? Papa?' protested Karapet indignantly. 'It had nothing to do with him. Nothing whatever. It was *my* bad luck entirely, not *his*!'

As we left the room we could hear the Armenian telling the Rabbit: 'It began on Walpurgis Night, 1313. The witch of Ararat. . . .'

4: Nemesis Keeps Her Lead

Admittedly, Papa's misfortunes distracted H.H. momentarily from his own, for next to winning, nothing gave him greater pleasure than to see Papa lose.

But the duplicate, even with the Rabbit as his partner, didn't shake Nemesis from his back.

The bad run continued and after a gloomy dinner the next day, the Hog again gave vent to his feelings.

A Devastating Lead

'That odious Greek,' he began. 'What he did to me this afternoon! And to think that we had against us the Rabbit and the Walrus, the most sought-after opponents in the western hemisphere. Now take that 4 ♠ contract. . . .'

This was the hand that had so incensed the Hog:

Dealer East: Both Vulnerable

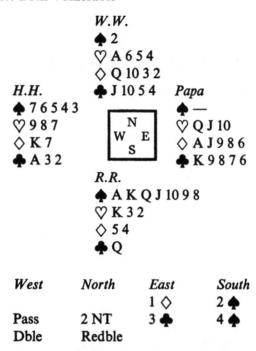

W.W.
♠ 2
♡ A 6 5 4
◇ Q 10 3 2
♣ J 10 5 4

H.H.
♠ 7 6 5 4 3
♡ 9 8 7
◇ K 7
♣ A 3 2

Papa
♠ —
♡ Q J 10
◇ A J 9 8 6
♣ K 9 8 7 6

R.R.
♠ A K Q J 10 9 8
♡ K 3 2
◇ 5 4
♣ Q

West	North	East	South
		1 ◇	2 ♠
Pass	2 NT	3 ♣	4 ♠
Dble	Redble		

A better man than the Rueful Rabbit might have been doubled by a player with the West cards. Assessing the Rabbit's declarer-value to the defence at two tricks—a conservative estimate by any standard—H.H. had, therefore, a good deal to spare.

W.W's redouble was based on brute strength. 'With ten points and two tens,' he said, tabling his cards, 'I have a lot more than partner can possibly expect.'

'Which ten points?' asked Oscar in some perplexity.

The Walrus explained that he was worth seven high-card points and three more for the singleton. He had always found the 5–3–1 scale for voids, singletons and doubletons to be eminently sound and reliable.

'Is a singleton trump worth a full three points?' inquired the Toucan in a low voice. 'I mean er. . . .'

Before he could complete the sentence and while dummy's

cards were still being arranged, it transpired that the opening lead, the ♣ Q had been made by declarer himself.

For obvious reasons, no sane partner redoubled when R.R. was at the wheel. Caught in the whirl of a new experience, with the Hog snarling at him from one side and Papa glaring at him from the other, the Rabbit lost, momentarily, his precarious sense of balance. Hence the strange spectacle of declarer firing the first shot at his own contract.

When the jeers had subsided and the offending card was back in declarer's hand, the Hideous Hog opened proceedings with the ◇ K. Then came the ◇ 7. Papa won the trick with the knave and I could hear his brain ticking loudly. His side had taken two tricks and it was clear from R.R's comic opening that he had a singleton ♣ Q. It looked as if the best defence would be to promote a trump in partner's hand. Yet if he now played the ◇ A, the Rabbit might ruff high, and discard a losing club later on dummy's ◇ Q. What if the Hog ruffed? There was no point in promoting a trump in his hand just so that he might waste it on one of declarer's losers.

Alternatively, if the Greek led a low diamond, R.R. would throw on it his ♣ Q and again there would be no advantage to the defence.

The way out of the impasse came to Papa in a flash. First he put down his ♣ K, neatly picking up R.R's singleton queen. Then he shot a low diamond through declarer's gizzard. The Rueful Rabbit ruffed with the eight and proceeded to draw trumps. This was the four-card end-position.

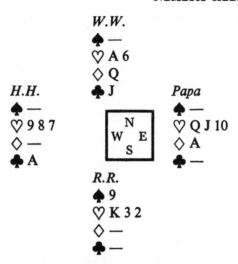

W.W.
♠ —
♡ A 6
◇ Q
♣ J

H.H.
♠ —
♡ 9 8 7
◇ —
♣ A

Papa
♠ —
♡ Q J 10
◇ A
♣ —

R.R.
♠ 9
♡ K 3 2
◇ —
♣ —

R.R. screwed his eyes as he tried counting the trumps. Was there one more lurking somewhere? It was so easy to miss a small card in the general mêlée. Taking no chances he played the ♠ 9.

To keep the ♣ A, the Hog was forced to part with a heart. 'Ah, well,' said the Rabbit letting go dummy's ♣ J. 'Papa isn't likely to throw his ♣ A away, so the knave isn't much use to me.' To retain the ◇ A the Greek, too, had to part with a heart. Much to his suprise the Rabbit's ♡ 2 won the last trick.

'Saboteur!' cried the Hog. 'Quisling! Fifth Columnist! What possessed you to lead out of the blue that ♣ K?' Papa evaded the question with a series of highly expressive gestures.

'In a redoubled contract, partner,' said the Walrus reproachfully, 'you should pay enough attention not to lead out of turn. No harm was done, as it happens, but it might have made all the difference.'

The Rueful Rabbit hung his head in shame. He knew that he had made himself ridiculous and he was badly rattled.

Nemesis Strikes Again

On the last rubber before dinner, fate struck another cruel blow at the Hideous Hog. Walter the Walrus, sitting West, dealt and opened 1 ♡, which the Secretary Bird, in the North position, doubled. The Rabbit, East, unaccustomed to holding poor cards, was paying little attention. He had picked up: ♠ 6 5 ♡ 3 2 ♢ 5 4 3 2 ♣ 5 4 3 2 and his mind was far away. A few minutes later, he found himself defending a contract of 3 ♠.

S.B.
♠ K J 10 9
♡ J 8 7 6
♢ K Q J
♣ A K

R.R.
♠ 6 5
♡ 3 2
♢ 5 4 3 2
♣ 5 4 3 2

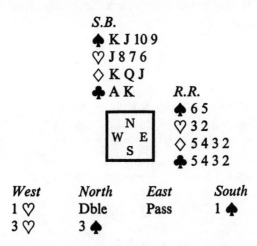

West	North	East	South
1 ♡	Dble	Pass	1 ♠
3 ♡	3 ♠		

The Walrus led the ♡ Q, then the ♡ K. All followed. After taking the ♢ A, W.W. continued with the ♡ A.

'There's a card on the floor,' said a young kibitzer suddenly. Picking up the seven of spades and holding it face upwards, he handed it to the Rabbit.

'That's an exposed card,' announced S.B., determined as ever to insist on the letter of the law.

'No, no,' broke in the Hog hastily. 'Walter would have to be seven feet tall to see it. Besides, it was such a very small card and er. . . .' His voice trailed off.

Walter looked up suspiciously. Why was the Hog being magnanimous? Clearly, because it was against his interest to enforce the penalty. Therefore, it was up to W.W. to take sides against himself, so to speak, and to insist on paying the price in full, for what was good for the Hog was bad for the Walrus and vice versa.

'I am taller than you think,' he protested. 'I did, I mean I could have seen that card. Had I stood up, I could even. . . .'

'Oh! Here you are,' cried the exasperated Rabbit, banging the seven of trumps on his partner's ace. 'All these arguments are so

unnecessary and none of it makes a scrap of difference anyway.'
The Hog overruffed the seven with the queen and led a trump.
Winning with the ace, W.W. played another heart. The Rabbit
ruffed dummy's knave with the ♠ 6 and this for some reason held
the trick. R.R. did not examine such things too closely. This was
the deal:

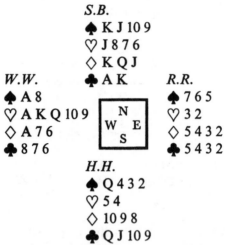

S.B.
♠ K J 10 9
♡ J 8 7 6
◇ K Q J
♣ A K

W.W.
♠ A 8
♡ A K Q 10 9
◇ A 7 6
♣ 8 7 6

R.R.
♠ 7 6 5
♡ 3 2
◇ 5 4 3 2
♣ 5 4 3 2

H.H.
♠ Q 4 3 2
♡ 5 4
◇ 10 9 8
♣ Q J 10 9

'I shall get my own back on her, have no fear,' said the Hideous
Hog menacingly, 'but that afternoon Nemesis did her worst. In
less than two hours I was thirty points down.'

'Surely you are exaggerating,' interposed Oscar the Owl, our
Senior Kibitzer at the Griffins. 'I was watching, as you know, and
I did not get the impression that it was all quite so one-sided.'

'Here's my card,' replied H.H. with hauteur. 'Add it up yourself.'

'Well,' said O.O., after checking the figures. 'I make you only
minus ten.'

'Precisely,' agreed the Hog, 'and I would have you know it that
it was a quarter to eight. By that time I expect to be at least plus
twenty. Some of you people don't understand simple arithmetic.
No wonder', he added, 'that you find bridge so difficult.'

5. En Route for the Moon

'Well played R.R.!' said Oscar the Owl incredulously.

'Surpri . . . er remarkably well played,' echoed Peregrine the Penguin.

There had been some hitch in the movement and while the Tournament Director straightened things out, we had time to admire the Rabbit's display of skill on this board in the Gala Individual.

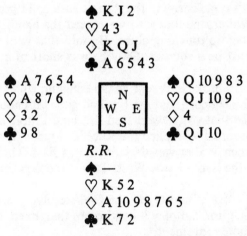

```
                    ♠ K J 2
                    ♡ 4 3
                    ◇ K Q J
                    ♣ A 6 5 4 3
  ♠ A 7 6 5 4                    ♠ Q 10 9 8 3
  ♡ A 8 7 6         N            ♡ Q J 10 9
  ◇ 3 2          W     E         ◇ 4
  ♣ 9 8             S            ♣ Q J 10
                    R.R.
                    ♠ —
                    ♡ K 5 2
                    ◇ A 10 9 8 7 6 5
                    ♣ K 7 2
```

contract: 5 ◇ by South

West, a nondescript character with big ears and a vacuous expression, opened a trump against the Rabbit's 5 ◇.

Playing with supreme confidence, the Rueful Rabbit led dummy's ♠ K to the second trick, throwing from his hand a small club. Thereafter it was plain sailing. West played his other trump, but it made no difference. The Rabbit ruffed out the clubs and crossing over to dummy with a diamond, discarded two hearts on the two long clubs.

His ears glowed with pleasure at the unaccustomed compliments from the kibitzers.

'I thought I'd got it right,' chittered R.R. happily. 'He said that the ♠ K must be played before drawing trumps, because East might have the ♠ A—only we know he hasn't, of course—and then there must be another entry to dummy to do the same thing with the ♠ J, because he said. . . .'

'Who said what?' asked Oscar, who was growing a little exasperated.

'The Hog,' replied the Rabbit, 'that's how he played it and . . .'

'Do you mean . . .' began Oscar, but one of the players, who had opened the travelling score sheet, interrupted him.

'Amazing,' he exclaimed. 'Someone contrived to go *two* down in 5 ◇. It's impossible. There must be a mistake. . . .'

'No, no, it's quite correct,' the Rabbit hastened to reassure him. 'That was Walter, the first time we played the hand. He drew all the trumps before touching clubs. He said that with such a long suit there must be a squeeze. Only he was short of a menace. At least. . . .'

'Stop! Stop!' broke in Peregrine the Penguin, who felt as official kibitzer at the Unicorn that matters had gone far enough. 'Are we to understand that you have played this board three times?'

'No, no, not really,' replied the Rabbit. 'I mean, not at all. The first time, when Walter was declarer, I was East. Then, when the Hog played the hand, I was West. This is the first time I've been South.'

'But surely R.R.,' said Oscar the Owl sternly, 'you must know that no competitor can play a hand more than once. Now you've upset the whole movement. . . .'

'Oh, but don't you see,' broke in the Rabbit excitedly, 'I am number One. I am the pivot. I don't even have to move, only I gave up my seat to that old gentleman in the corner with the gouty foot and I have followed the board instead. It's quite all right really. In my case, you see, they probably didn't think that it would matter much if I saw the hands before, that is. . . .'

At this point the Tournament Director made an announcement. After expressing regret for the inconvenience which it would cause competitors, he ruled that the last two boards should be cancelled. With a look of unmistakable hostility towards R.R., he added: 'Will the players, *all* the players, resume the positions in which they sat for Round One.'

'Ah, well, these things happen. One must take the rough with the smooth,' I heard Papa remark philosophically. He was at the next table and I gathered that things had not been going his way.

'It's a diabolical scandal,' roared the Hog from the other end of the room. 'They've robbed me of two tops!'

With downcast eyes, his sense of guilt weighing heavily upon him, the Rabbit slunk ruefully away. He was still badly rattled ten minutes later, when it fell to him to be the Hog's partner against Papa and Colin the Corgi.

A Future in Fright?

At game to North-South Papa dealt and opened 3 ♠. Sitting between the Greek and the Rabbit I could see:

```
                        R.R.
                        ♠ Q 10 8
                        ♡ Q 10 9 8 4 3
                        ◇ 3 2
        Papa            ♣ 3 2
        ♠ J 9 7 6 5 4 3
        ♡ A             ┌─────────┐
        ◇ 9 8 7 6 5     │    N    │
        ♣ —             │  W   E  │
                        │    S    │
                        └─────────┘
```

This was the auction:

West	North	East	South
Papa	R.R.	C.C.	H.H.
3 ♠	Pass	Pass	3 NT
Pass	4 ♡	Dble	4 ♠
Dble	Pass	Pass	5 ♠
Pass	Pass!		

It is only fair to the Rabbit to note that before passing the Hog's cue bid he shivered and trembled all over. His ears quivered. His nose twitched and beads of perspiration formed on his forehead. He knew well enough, as he confessed later, that he had been called upon to choose between the minors, the two unbid suits. But though a soft, high-pitched squeak formed at the back of his throat, it did not amount to a bid. A minute or two later, he found the strength to murmur 'No bid'. When it was all over, he told me in confidence: 'I just could not undertake to make twelve tricks on a two-card trump suit headed by the deuce and the three.'

The Hideous Hog did not wait for Colin the Corgi to pass before launching on a vigorous speech in which he neither repeated himself nor stooped to use a single Parliamentary expression.

Meanwhile, Papa was thinking. What should he open? For a player with seven trumps, the task of selecting a lead against a cue bid at the five level rarely presents insuperable problems. Papa was not worried and he would have been the first to admit that it mattered little whether the contract was beaten by six tricks or by seven or only by five. A cold top calls for no further refrigeration, but there are ways of prolonging the pleasure and Papa paused sadistically, resolved to extract every ounce of joy from the agony that awaited the Hog.

Finally, 'to look at the table', as he put it, the Greek led the ♡ A.

The Hog, still in full flood, trumped with the ♠ 2 in his hand, and followed with the ♢ A, then the ♢ K. When Colin threw a club on the second diamond, H.H. paused, leaving unfinished a pithy sentence about craven cretinous curs. A few seconds later he spread his hand with a cry of triumph and claimed the contract. At the third trick he could place every card. Since Colin had one diamond only, Papa was marked with five; and since Colin could not ruff, the Greek could be credited with seven spades. His thirteenth card was the ace of hearts which he had led.

This was the full deal:

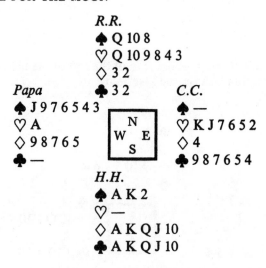

R.R.
♠ Q 10 8
♡ Q 10 9 8 4 3
◇ 3 2
♣ 3 2

Papa
♠ J 9 7 6 5 4 3
♡ A
◇ 9 8 7 6 5
♣ —

C.C.
♠ —
♡ K J 7 6 5 2
◇ 4
♣ 9 8 7 6 5 4

H.H.
♠ A K 2
♡ —
◇ A K Q J 10
♣ A K Q J 10

No one asked H.H. how he proposed to play the hand. He took pains to explain, however, that he intended to lead his five diamonds slowly, one by one. Papa's part in the proceedings would be confined to following suit. At that point, H.H. would have six tricks and no one could stop him from making five more on a cross ruff.

'Let me just run through it again,' he began with a dulcet smile at Papa, when the Rabbit broke in with an apologetic noise. 'I . . . I . . . I mean . . . I . . .' The sounds were not very clear.

Fortunately, the Hog was in a magnanimous mood. 'As I have always said, you were perfectly right to pass, and anyway,' he added, 'I won't hold it against you.'

A Surfeit of Winners

As the evening wore on the rumour gained ground that the Rabbit, who was bearing a charmed life, stood a good chance of winning the first prize, the coveted estate on the moon. The donor was a distinguished trans-Atlantic property tycoon, President of Outer Space Development Inc., of Baton Rouge, La., who was sponsoring the tournament.

The Grand Prix was a 10,000 acre estate on the moon, 'quiet,

D

secluded, unspoilt by man, superbly situated between the Sea of Tribulation and the Lake of Calamity,' in the words of the glossy brochure.

H.H. and R.R. were well ahead of the rest of the field when they met in a fateful clash on the last board.

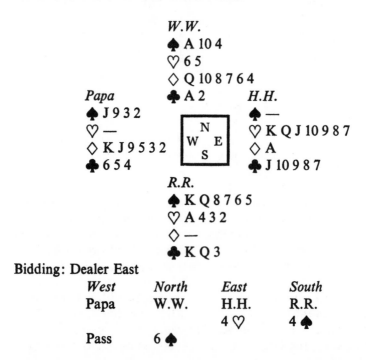

W.W.
♠ A 10 4
♡ 6 5
◇ Q 10 8 7 6 4
♣ A 2

Papa
♠ J 9 3 2
♡ —
◇ K J 9 5 3 2
♣ 6 5 4

H.H.
♠ —
♡ K Q J 10 9 8 7
◇ A
♣ J 10 9 8 7

R.R.
♠ K Q 8 7 6 5
♡ A 4 3 2
◇ —
♣ K Q 3

Bidding: Dealer East

West	North	East	South
Papa	W.W.	H.H.	R.R.
		4 ♡	4 ♠
Pass	6 ♠		

Papa nearly doubled the Rabbit's 4 ♠, but passed 6 ♠ with a look of studied boredom. The ◇ 9 was the best false card he could find for an opening lead.

The Rabbit ruffed, crossed to dummy with a club and ruffed another diamond. Then he played off the ♣ K and ♣ Q, discarding a heart from dummy, and sitting back took stock. Usually he left this part of it to the end-game, but on this last decisive board R.R. was on his mettle, thinking well ahead.

He could see six trump tricks—he did not expect suits to break 4–0—three clubs and the ♡ A. The addition, after two recounts, came to ten and he needed twelve. Even a heart ruff would raise the total to only eleven and that did not look too promising. Papa probably had no heart, since he had not led one, and might start ruffing himself.

The Rabbit knew from bitter experience that when declarer was short of a trick—in the Hog's case it could even be three tricks—things could be put right by means of a squeeze. And the first step, according to all the text books, was to begin by losing a trick. Clausewitz said it. The Hog said it. Everyone said it and they all called it *'the rectification of the count'*.

The difficulty in this case was that the Rabbit had only winners. How, then, could he lose a trick? He thought of ducking a trump, but that was too contrived, besides looking ostentatious. He could not lose a diamond, since he had none, and he had already disposed of the clubs. That only left hearts. So ruefully the Rabbit played the two away from his ace. Papa threw a diamond and the Hog won. Having nothing better to do he returned another heart to which the Rabbit played low. Papa once more parted with a diamond and dummy's ♠ 4 took the trick.

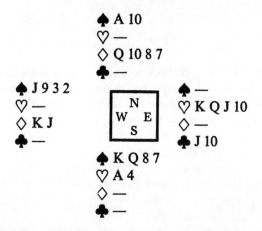

Coming back to the closed hand with a diamond ruff, R.R. led his ♡ A. If Papa ruffed, dummy would overruff, and he would be left with the ◇ K to follow to another diamond from dummy, which R.R. would ruff with the ♠ 8. If Papa threw his ◇ K, he would be no better off. The A 10 of trumps would remain intact on the table, poised over him, to deal with the Rabbit's ♡ 4.

'Didn't it occur to you,' cried the Hog, 'to ruff the first heart and to lead a trump?'

'To trump your trick and lose in the process a trump trick of my own?' countered Papa indignantly.

With seven cards left the position would have been:

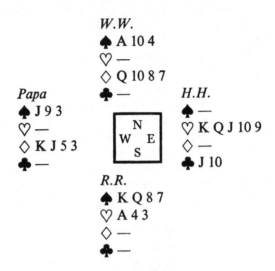

W.W.
♠ A 10 4
♡ —
◇ Q 10 8 7
♣ —

Papa
♠ J 9 3
♡ —
◇ K J 5 3
♣ —

H.H.
♠ —
♡ K Q J 10 9
◇ —
♣ J 10

R.R.
♠ K Q 8 7
♡ A 4 3
◇ —
♣ —

The Rabbit would win Papa's spade return with the ♠ 7 and would ruff a heart in dummy, then a diamond in his hand with the eight of trumps. But no matter in which order he played his remaining cards he would end up with a loser—either the ♡ A, if he kept it to the last or the ♡ 4. Papa would ruff the ♡ A, but would otherwise sit back, discarding diamonds and waiting for a trump trick to come to him or for his partner to make a heart.

'I see it all quite clearly,' said R.R. eagerly. 'I rectified the count by losing a winner and you could have done even better Papa, by turning two winners into losers.'

'You have no more idea of what you are talking about than the man in the moon,' replied Papa irritably. And that, in view of the announcement which the Tournament Director was to make shortly proved to be a truly prophetic remark.

6. Feats of Self-Destruction

'Of course, I don't believe in luck,' snorted the Hog contemptuously, 'though we all know, mind you, that it exists.'

We were sipping Madeira at the Unicorn Bar after an arduous session, and the Hideous Hog, who prided himself on being an indefatigable winner, was in carefree mood.

'The Rueful Rabbit is a case in point,' began Peregrine the Penguin.

'Or Walter the Walrus,' interrupted Oscar the Owl.

'No, no,' said H.H., shaking his head vigorously, 'apart from being the two worst players on the planet, they have nothing in common. For one thing, the Walrus does not play bridge. He counts it. He lives on points and peters and things, and he is only so bad because he insists on doing his best, which is, needless to say, abysmal. Not so the Rabbit, who rarely concentrates long enough to know what he is doing. Why, he has even been known to play the right card. No malice in it, mind you, but it makes him quite unpredictable. Now take that last rubber. . . .'

The Emeritus Professor of Bio-Sophistry, known to us all as the Secretary Bird on account of his appearance, had cut Walter the Walrus against the Rueful Rabbit and the Hideous Hog. This was one of the early deals:

S.B.
♠ —
♡ A 5 4 3 2
◇ A K 9 8
♣ A K 9 8

R.R.   *H.H.*
♠ J 9 7 6 4   ♠ 5 3
♡ 8 7   ♡ K Q J 10 9
◇ 7 6 5   N   ◇ Q J 10
♣ 7 6 5   W   E   ♣ Q J 10
                 S

W.W.
♠ A K Q 10 8 2
♡ 6
◇ 4 3 2
♣ 4 3 2

South	West	North	East
			1 ♡
1 ♠	Pass	3 ◇	Pass
3 ♠	Pass	4 ♣	Pass
4 ♠	Dble	Redble	

The Professor explained afterwards the reasons for his redouble. With his rockcrusher and three controls—four, in a manner of speaking—the only possible losers would be in the trump suit, and even if the Walrus had no better than K Q J x x x x, he surely could not contrive to lose more than three of them.

Alternatively, he fully expected to go down. After all, the other side had opened the bidding. But the redouble would cost a mere 100, while if opponents panicked into five of anything, it could lead to the most luscious massacre of the year.

The Rabbit, who remembered the bidding, opened the ♡ 8. The Walrus won with the ace, ruffed a heart with the ♠ 2 in his hand and crossing to the table with a diamond, led another heart. His idea was, evidently, to make his 10 8 2 of trumps by ruffing in the closed hand and he was about to play the ♠ 8 on the ♡ 3, when R.R., in sudden distress, gurgled and gasped. A piece of chocolate almond biscuit, at which he had been nibbling, was misrouted on the way down the oesophagus and the Rabbit, red in the face, spluttered and choked in an effort to redirect it. As he struggled, his fingers let go the cards and they came fluttering down on the the table, mostly face upwards.

'Drink some water,' suggested Peregrine.

'Slap him on the back,' advised Oscar.

'Hold your breath,' said the Walrus.

'Do you know your rights, partner?' asked Secretary Bird.

The ♠ 6 and ♠ 4, the two remaining diamonds and the three small clubs were all exposed cards. Only the ♠ J 9 7 had come down face downwards.

'Pick them up. Pick them up,' said W.W. chivalrously as R.R. began to regain his breath.

'You have a duty to your partner,' insisted S.B. in a steely voice. He did not like people to trifle with the laws or to be generous at his expense.

'Have no fear,' said the Rabbit, now breathing more freely. 'I wouldn't dream of profiting by Walter's magnanimity.'

'Pick them up,' persisted the Walrus. 'In any case, I won't call them.'

'Then,' replied the Rabbit with a courtly bow, 'I will select them myself to your best advantage.'

'Two can play at that game,' retorted W.W. Replacing the ♠ 8, he ruffed the little heart with the ♠ A. In almost the same movement, the Rabbit placed on it triumphantly his ♠ 6.

The Hog, who had been strangely silent, now cleared his throat.

'R.R. is quite right,' he said, grunting silkily. 'He cannot take advantage of Walter's *beau geste*. It wouldn't be cricket.' S.B. looked at him suspiciously.

The Walrus went back to dummy with a second diamond and ruffed another heart, blatantly, with the king. Defiantly, the Rabbit put on it the ♠ 4.

'And now,' observed H.H., 'since no card of interest remains exposed, honour I think, has been satisfied. Don't you agree, Professor?'

S.B. hissed malevolently. Some swindle was afoot. But what could it be? The Walrus cashed his two top clubs leaving this position:

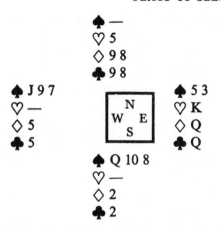

```
              ♠ —
              ♡ 5
              ◇ 9 8
              ♣ 9 8
♠ J 9 7                      ♠ 5 3
♡ —          ┌─────────┐    ♡ K
◇ 5          │   N     │    ◇ Q
♣ 5          │ W   E   │    ♣ Q
             │   S     │
             └─────────┘
              ♠ Q 10 8
              ♡ —
              ◇ 2
              ♣ 2
```

He led a third club to the Hog's queen. The five of trumps came back. Walter played the eight and the Rabbit, winning with the nine, exited with his diamond. Whether H.H. returned the spade or the heart, the defence was bound to win another trick. One down.

'I have never seen either of you play so well before,' said that facetious young man, Colin the Corgi, who had been kibitzing unobtrusively.

'Could I have made it?' asked W.W.

'Not so long as R.R. defended in *your* best interests,' C.C. and H.H. assured him in unison.

C.C. proceeded to explain that without the two underruffs, the Rabbit's last five cards would have all been trumps. He would have had to ruff the third club and to lead a trump into declarer's Q 10 8. Walter would have led his ◇ 2 and once more R.R. would have been compelled to ruff and so lead a trump into the Q 10.

'One overtrick,' pointed out the Hog. 'So you were right to redouble after all, Professor. You were within the fraction of a biscuit of a really good score. He! He!'

Smother de se

On the next hand the Walrus bid and made 1 NT. After that nothing much happened for a while. First one side went down, then the other and several hands were thrown in. Then, just as the Walrus had completed the count down from three, his partner, S.B., opened 2 ♣. This was the deal.

Dealer South: Love All

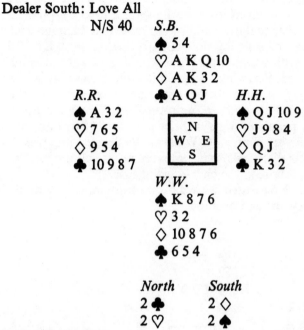

N/S 40

S.B.
♠ 5 4
♡ A K Q 10
◇ A K 3 2
♣ A Q J

R.R.
♠ A 3 2
♡ 7 6 5
◇ 9 5 4
♣ 10 9 8 7

H.H.
♠ Q J 10 9
♡ J 9 8 4
◇ Q J
♣ K 3 2

W.W.
♠ K 8 7 6
♡ 3 2
◇ 10 8 7 6
♣ 6 5 4

North	South
2 ♣	2 ◇
2 ♡	2 ♠

R.R. led the ♣ 10.

'I've given up 100 honours for you, but there's nothing like making safety doubly sure,' announced S.B. tabling his hand. Looking even more bemused than usual, the Walrus muttered something about 'twenty-six and not in game brr . . . grr.' Then he noticed the score and blushed guiltily.

On the opening lead W.W. took the losing club finesse. Coming in with the ♣ K, the Hog returned the ♠ Q, then the ♠ J, declarer playing low both times. A club to dummy's queen was followed by the three top hearts. On the third heart the Walrus threw a club and on the ♣ A, which came next, he parked a diamond. His attention was now drawn to dummy's top diamonds, but the Hog's queen, coming down on the ace, sounded a warning and Walter the Walrus took stock. Six tricks were stacked neatly in front of him—two clubs, three hearts and the ◇ A. He needed only two more. The ◇ K, so long as H.H. did not ruff it, would be one of them. A trump would produce the other. To give himself every chance the Walrus led dummy's last heart. If the Hog showed out, he would ruff it—with the ♠ K if need be—and exit with a trump. After that he would surely come to a diamond trick.

When, instead of showing out, H.H. turned up with the ♡ J, Walter parted with a diamond. What would the Rabbit discard? His nose quivered. Screwing his eyes and compressing his lips, he tried desperately to remember if any clubs were still out. Was there, perhaps, a little one lurking somewhere? He could not be sure. So many people nowadays threw high cards and kept small ones. It was all very confusing. What finally decided him was the thought that his diamonds were probably not much use anyway. He let one go, retaining the club—just in case.

The Hideous Hog exited with the ◇ J to dummy's ◇ K, this being the three-card end position.

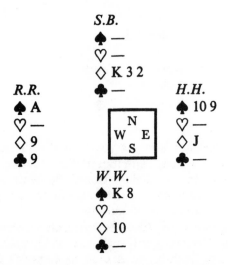

S.B.
♠ —
♡ —
◇ K 3 2
♣ —

R.R.
♠ A
♡ —
◇ 9
♣ 9

H.H.
♠ 10 9
♡ —
◇ J
♣ —

W.W.
♠ K 8
♡ —
◇ 10
♣ —

After the ◇ K came the ◇ 2. The Hog ruffed with the nine and Walter was helpless. If he overruffed with the king, the Rabbit would ruff with the ace. If he underruffed, the Rabbit would throw a club.

'I must make a note of the hand,' said H.H., stretching across the table for the Rabbit's silver pencil.

'You're going to work it out?' inquired W.W. eagerly. 'You think that, maybe, I could have made it—that is, double dummy?'

'Well, not exactly,' purred the Hideous Hog, 'I was wondering how you made certain of six losers against any possible distribution.'

The Walrus was beginning to suspect that he had not played the hand to the best advantage.

'A smother play,' went on H.H., baring his teeth in a friendly grimace, 'is hard enough to perform against opponents. Against oneself, as a sort of *felo de se*—or should it be smother *de se*?—it is surely unique. I can think of only one other player who has the technique, the er flair. . . .'

The Rabbit winced. The Hideous Hog was still gloating happily after the cards had been dealt again.

Dirty Looks

The rubber came to an end soon afterwards. Papa, who then joined the table, displacing the Emeritus Professor of Bio-Sophistry, cut the Rabbit against the Hog and the Walrus. Papa made 4 ♡ on the first hand. On the next, the Greek found himself in 3 NT. I was sitting behind the Hideous Hog.

R.R. (dummy)
♠ 7 6
♡ A Q J 9 8 7
◇ K 5
♣ 5 4 3

```
    N
  W   E
    S
```

H.H.
♠ A 10 3 2
♡ K 10
◇ Q J 10 9 8
♣ K 2

South	West	North	East
			1 ♣
1 ◇	1 ♡	Pass	3 ♣
Pass	3 ♡	Pass	3 NT

H.H. opened the proceedings with the ◇ Q. The Greek won
with the king on the table and continued with the ♣ 5. Walter the
Walrus produced the seven and Papa played the queen. Looking
a trifle bored, I thought, the Hideous Hog followed with the two.
Just at this moment, Robin, the card-room steward came up to
tell me: 'An urgent call for you, sir, from Paris.'

Not until we had gathered together in the bar, an hour later,
did I hear the sequel to that defence.

'What happened?' I asked the Hog.

'Just a routine example of perfect defence,' he explained. 'You
understand, of course, why I played low to that club, unguarding
my king?'

'You . . .' I began.

'Not at all,' interrupted H.H., 'all I did was to place every card
at trick one and arrange for the unbreakable contract to be
broken.'

I had nearly formed a syllable, but he was a fraction too quick
for me. 'To account for his jump rebid,' went on H.H., 'Papa
would need at least six clubs, if not seven, and he obviously had
the ♣ A Q. If it was a seven-card suit, he could not lose anyway,
but if he had six only, he could not muster on top more than
eight tricks—five clubs, if he lost one to my king, two diamonds
and the ♡ A. So he would be driven to take the heart finesse, and,
if he did, all six would fall conveniently into his lap. My only hope
was to make him think that the ♣ K was on the right side. Then,
to repeat the finesse, he would cross to dummy with his only
remaining entry, the ♡ A. Coming in with the ♣ K, I would
clear my diamonds and would then wait patiently for the curtain.
I rather thought, by the way, that the bidding and the play, too,
for that matter pointed to a singleton heart in the closed hand,
and I was right, of course. I would be the last man, as you know,'
added the Hog, 'to sing my own praises, but I must confess that it
was a pretty defence.'

I agreed. 'After that, you certainly deserved to win the rubber.
Did you?' I asked.

'*We* did not win the rubber. *He* lost it. On that very hand,
what's more,' replied H.H. bitterly.

Seeing my look of consternation, the Hideous Hog jotted down
the four hands.

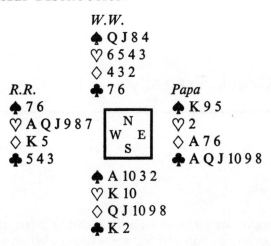

W.W.
♠ Q J 8 4
♡ 6 5 4 3
◇ 4 3 2
♣ 7 6

R.R.
♠ 7 6
♡ A Q J 9 8 7
◇ K 5
♣ 5 4 3

Papa
♠ K 9 5
♡ 2
◇ A 7 6
♣ A Q J 10 9 8

♠ A 10 3 2
♡ K 10
◇ Q J 10 9 8
♣ K 2

'Naturally,' went on H.H., 'Papa followed the road to self-destruction which I had mapped out for him. He led a heart, looked with contempt at my ten—such an obvious false card, it seemed—and he duly went up with the ace. Then came a club, as prescribed by me and then . . . guess!'

'The Walrus revoked?' I hazarded.

'He did far worse,' replied the Hog. 'You may remember that he followed to the first club with the seven. He now produced the six. Yes, he was signalling a doubleton! Now no one would hold a thing like that against the Rabbit for he does not discriminate much between different cards. But W.W. counts every pip and it would no more occur to him to deceive declarer than to owe his partner a ten in a no trump bid. So,' went on the Hog, 'Papa gave me a dirty look, that is, a dirtier look than he usually gives me, and triumphantly dropped my ♣ K.'

Imparting melancholy to a doleful snort, as only he could do, the Hog added: 'That Walrus! I am sure he signals to himself when he plays patience. Tcha!'

7. A Greek Tragedy

'I can forgive the Hideous Hog for gloating. After all, he can't help it. Let him whoop with joy every time he brings off the Bath Coup or any other technical masterpiece. But why must I submit to an indecent exhibition of glee whenever some revolting atrocity of his goes unpunished? Why should he be allowed to pretend that all his howlers are works of art?'

There was burning indignation in Papa's voice. The Hog's long, bad run had been succeeded by a burst of good cards and he was pressing his luck to the limit, often at Papa's expense.

Unlike so many millionaires, Themistocles Papadopoulos could lose small sums of money with comparative equanimity. But he did not like to be ridiculed whenever fortune frowned on him. In short, he could put up with the moans of the losers, but not with the jeers of the winners, still less with sneers from the kibitzers. The Hog offended in every rôle.

'That Hideous Hog, you know,' went on the Greek bitterly, 'laughs when he sees a portly old gentleman trip over a banana skin, not as we all do, because it's an incongruous spectacle, but because the old gentleman might break his leg. It's that which strikes him as so uproariously funny.'

A hand that had greatly incensed Papa had come up early that afternoon.

Papa had Walter the Walrus as his partner. The situation looked promising, so the Hog seated himself behind the Greek, waiting hopefully for some misfortune to befall him. This was the first hand of the rubber.

Dealer East: Love All   *W.W.*

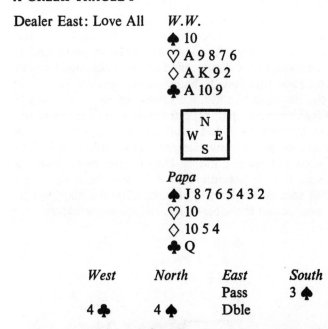

♠ 10
♡ A 9 8 7 6
◊ A K 9 2
♣ A 10 9

Papa
♠ J 8 7 6 5 4 3 2
♡ 10
◊ 10 5 4
♣ Q

West	North	East	South
		Pass	3 ♠
4 ♣	4 ♠	Dble	

The opening lead was the ♡ Q which Papa captured with dummy's ace. The ten of spades followed. The Toucan won the trick with the queen of trumps and continued with the ♡ K. The Rabbit's contribution to the trump trick had been the ♣ 7.

The Greek frowned. His long, sensitive fingers beat a nervous tattoo on the table as he surveyed his prospects. After ruffing the ♡ K he would still have three more trumps than the Toucan and he would need, therefore, four entries in dummy for the triple coup on which the contract would now depend. With three cards left, the position would have to be:

A K 9

J 8 7

with the lead in dummy.

At first sight, there were only three entries to the table, though fortunately, prospects were not quite as bleak as they seemed. As

Papa explained later, every card was marked. T.T. had passed as dealer and he had shown up already with the ♠ A K Q and the ♡ K. He was unlikely, therefore, to have another point and it was an odds-on chance that the double finesse in diamonds would succeed, giving Papa that fourth, badly needed entry.

Sizing up the situation quickly, the Greek led the ◇ 4 towards dummy. The Rabbit came up unexpectedly with the knave and the trick was taken by the king. A heart ruff brought Papa back to his hand and once more he led a low diamond to the table. The Rueful Rabbit produced the queen, killing that fourth entry and the contract with it. Was it possible that R.R. had been dealt the ◇ Q J bare? It seemed the only explanation for the play, but to make sure I went round the table to look at the other hands.

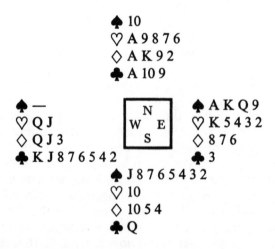

How was it that the Rabbit had found so inspired a defence? Papa gasped. Timothy, looking more than ever like a Toucan, his shiny red nose mirrored in the midnight blue of his glossy summer suit, bounced in his chair: 'I thought a forcing game was best,' he twittered excitedly. The Rabbit, conscious of his brilliance, beamed with pleasure.

Walter the Walrus glared reproachfully at Papa. 'Three points,' he said severely, 'hardly qualifies for an opening, for *any* sort of opening.'

'What made you go up with those diamond honours?' cried the

exasperated Greek. 'Had anyone else done it, it would have been bad enough, but that you of all people . . . why, why, why?'

'Perhaps, because I am not quite so bad as you all think,' replied the Rueful Rabbit with a jaunty twitch of his left ear. 'I was following the game closely, you know, and I could see what you were up to, ruffing those hearts and everything. You were eliminating, stripping me, all set to throw me in with a diamond so that I should have to play away from the ♣ K J. Well, I knew I had to keep an exit card and I did, didn't I?' The Rabbit's right ear twitched in sympathy with the left as he leant back triumphantly to sip his cherry brandy.

Papa threw up his hands in despair. He looked like some character in a Greek tragedy, pursued and overtaken by the Furies. 'Against inspired lunacy what can a man do?' he asked feebly. Then, turning on the Hog who was jeering contentedly, he cried out: 'You've been moaning about your bad luck for months, but this sort of thing could never happen to you!'

'No,' agreed H.H. with alacrity. 'I try to give myself the best chance. Of course, it requires a certain technique and. . . .'

'Are you suggesting . . .' broke in the Greek.

'Yes, I am,' snapped back H.H. 'You threw the hand away at trick two by leading a spade from dummy. Timothy gave you a chance by returning a heart, allowing you to shorten your trumps. But for that you would have had no hope, anyway. R.R. merely put right his partner's mistake and you really can't expect both defenders to co-operate with you.'

'But what . . .' spluttered Papa.

'At trick two you should have ruffed a heart. You could afford to lead trumps from your hand and if that crazy mixed-up Toucan had led another heart as part of his 'forcing game', you wouldn't have needed that extra entry to dummy.

'Of course,' added the Hog, 'you were lucky to find T.T. with five hearts, otherwise, it wouldn't have been so easy, so childishly simple to execute a triple trump coup. But then, you've always been a lucky player, Papa. If I had your luck. . . .'

8. A Top for Papa ?

In recent days the Hideous Hog has shed much of his former aversion to duplicate. At one time he had moral scruples. 'It's very wrong,' he used to say, 'that people should commit sins without paying for them, and what are matchpoints to a man of means?' Even when someone introduced a modest stake into the weekly duplicates at the Unicorn, the Hog refused to be mollified.

'People can't learn to be good losers on the cheap,' he explained. 'Besides, one must think of the winners, too. Without them, what would the losers do?'

Not long ago, Papa the Greek and one or two others began to raise the stakes and eventually H.H. gave in. 'They'd be upset if I didn't play,' he told me in confidence. 'They'd think there was something wrong with duplicate itself and, well, there may be something in it after all.'

That's how it was that last Thursday the Hideous Hog came to be playing at the Unicorn with Colin the Corgi as his partner. Quick at spotting the mistakes of others, C.C. is never at a loss for a biting remark or a telling grimace. He is still very young, of course, but he has all the makings of an expert.

On the first set of boards, exchanged with a relay table, H.H. and C.C. faced Papa and his friend Karapet, the Free Armenian.

Dealer East: Love All   *C.C.*

              ♠ J 10
              ♡ Q 2
              ◇ A K J 10 9 8
              ♣ J 10 2

```
      N
   W     E
      S
```

H.H.

     ♠ A K
     ♡ A J 8 5 4
     ◇ 7
     ♣ A 6 5 4 3

South	*West*	*North*	*East*
H.H.	Papa	C.C.	Karapet
			1 ♣
1 ♡	Pass	3 ◇	Pass
3 NT	ALL PASS		

Papa opened the ♣ 9 to the ten, queen, and ace and the Hog surveyed the scene. It was clear on the bidding that West had a blizzard. The diamond finesse could not, therefore, succeed, and unless the hearts split 3–3, declarer could count on eight tricks only—two spades, three hearts, two diamonds and the ♣ A.

'Only goes to show,' I heard Peregrine the Penguin, the Unicorn's Senior Kibitzer, tell Oscar the Owl, his opposite number at the Griffins. 'With all those points and a near-solid suit, the odds are that he'll go down. Communications. . . .'

'Odds?' broke in the Hideous Hog, who must have overheard the Penguin's remark. 'They are well over 100 per cent in my favour. I was looking for overtricks.' He looked around, also, for a glass *en prise*. Seeing none, he led the ◇ 7 to dummy's ace and continued with the king and knave, throwing from his hand the ♠ A and ♠ K.

Then, as the Armenian won the third diamond with the queen, the Hog tabled his hand.

'Try the ♡ K,' he advised Karapet, 'it's faintly spectacular and no worse than anything else.'

With every card marked on the bidding, H.H. could be certain that dummy would have an entry in whichever suit Karapet decided to return. This was the deal:

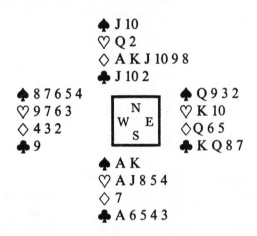

> ♠ J 10
> ♡ Q 2
> ◇ A K J 10 9 8
> ♣ J 10 2

♠ 8 7 6 5 4   ♠ Q 9 3 2
♡ 9 7 6 3   ♡ K 10
◇ 4 3 2   ◇ Q 6 5
♣ 9   ♣ K Q 8 7

> ♠ A K
> ♡ A J 8 5 4
> ◇ 7
> ♣ A 6 5 4 3

'These set hands,' said Papa scornfully, 'I knew it was all fixed as soon as I saw my lot. Some humorist at that relay table must have thought it no end of a joke to give *me* a Yarborough and let *him* throw away aces and kings.'

Too Brilliant

The next deal led to a spirited auction in which C.C. took full advantage of the favourable vulnerability.

Dealer South: E/W Vulnerable

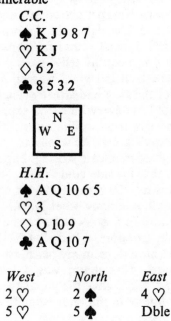

C.C.
♠ K J 9 8 7
♡ K J
♢ 6 2
♣ 8 5 3 2

H.H.
♠ A Q 10 6 5
♡ 3
♢ Q 10 9
♣ A Q 10 7

South	West	North	East
1 ♠	2 ♡	2 ♠	4 ♡
4 ♠	5 ♡	5 ♠	Dble
ALL PASS			

Intrepid bidding by Colin, but he knew that three down would show a profit if East-West could make 5 ♡.

Papa opened the ♡ 2 and H.H. looked at dummy with distaste bordering on disgust. What was this absurd sacrifice when he could see three tricks in defence, four if East had the ♣ K? The Hog was about to say something, probably quite a lot. Then, as he caught another glimpse of the ♡ 2, his snarl faded away. He gave the card a knowing wink and almost smiled.

'I wonder, Papa,' he said in his fruitiest voice, 'if that is the fourth highest of your longest suit. If not, what made you pick the deuce?' The Hideous Hog called for dummy's king, and when it held, he burst into triumphant laughter.

'So, it's another set hand, is it?' he said, mocking the Greek. 'And who set it? Why, you did, of course, Themistocles. Watch carefully,' went on H.H. addressing a bevy of kibitzers who had been attracted by the noise. He drew trumps in two rounds, ending in dummy, and swished the ♣ 8 into a horizontal position in the centre of the table. Karapet played low and the Hog ran it, with a gesture of defiance. The eight held. As Papa showed out, throwing a diamond, H.H. looked round for applause.

'How could you possibly tell?' gasped an astounded admirer.

'Don't ask or he'll tell you,' warned Colin the Corgi. But it was too late for the Hog had already cleared his throat.

'The ♡ 2 told me everything,' he explained tabling his hand. 'Yet oddly enough, it was quite an intelligent lead.' Raising his voice above Papa's growl, he went on:

'It's the result of duplicate scoring. Papa assumed, quite rightly as it happens, that his side could make game, so unless he could get us four down—700 against 620 or 650—he'd end up below average. After all, not many other North-South pairs would be so crazy as to bid up to 5 ♠ as Col . . . as er we did. Underplaying that ace wasn't, therefore, a bad shot. Had I misguessed, as any-one else would have done in my place, two club ruffs would have been his reward. That deuce was a brilliant suit signal—too brilliant, in fact, for it gave the game away, allowing me to take the deep club finesse in the knowledge that it must succeed.'

'But what made you go up with the ♡ K?' asked a kibitzer with baited breath.

'The score,' replied the Hideous Hog. Then, seeing the spec-tators properly mystified, he proceeded to explain. 'That's the beauty of duplicate. It would make little difference whether I went down two or three and I had nothing useful to discard on a set up heart, anyway. But if the king held the trick, it would be a top worth. . . .'

'Twelve pounds, I believe,' murmured the Corgi.

'Besides,' concluded H.H., 'I always expect Papa to do some-thing clever, and what would be so clever about leading from a queen?'

These were the four hands:

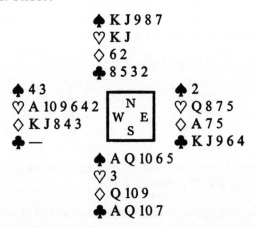

♠ K J 9 8 7
♡ K J
◇ 6 2
♣ 8 5 3 2

♠ 4 3
♡ A 10 9 6 4 2
◇ K J 8 4 3
♣ —

♠ 2
♡ Q 8 7 5
◇ A 7 5
♣ K J 9 6 4

♠ A Q 10 6 5
♡ 3
◇ Q 10 9
♣ A Q 10 7

I did not come across Papa again until just before the last round.
He appeared to be in close conference with Karapet as they
waited for their opponents and he beckoned me over. 'Have you
heard anything about that grand slam in spades?' he asked in a
whisper. 'Everybody is talking about it. Spoils the game, you
know, when these things leak out. People are so unscrupulous.
As I was telling Karapet just now, once they know that seven's
there, they'll bid it, on two finesses and a break. Standards these
days. . . .'

The Best Defence

Later, in the bar, waiting for the results, I joined Peregrine and
Oscar. The Penguin was showing the Owl this hand.

♠ K J 7 4
♡ J 10 9 8
◇ A 7 6 5
♣ A

'What do you lead', he asked us both, 'against 7 ♠?'
'But you haven't told us the bidding,' protested the Owl.
'Against what were they sacrificing?'
'It wasn't a sacrifice,' replied P.P. 'Moreover, the contract was

redoubled.' Noting with evident satisfaction our bewilderment, the Penguin wrote down this bidding sequence:

South (dealer)	North
1 ♠	3 ♡
4 ♡	5 ♣
5 ♡	6 ♣
6 NT	7 ♠

At this point West doubled and North redoubled.
'What do you lead?' persisted P.P.

'The ◇ A, I suppose,' returned O.O., 'and if I strike lucky, every time I come in, I'll lead another diamond to force declarer. Not that it can possibly matter which card I lead. Even two or three down would be the coldest of tops, so. . . .'

'On the contrary,' retorted the Penguin, 'the grand slam may hinge on the lead.' He showed us dummy, presenting this picture.

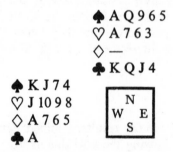

```
                ♠ A Q 9 6 5
                ♡ A 7 6 3
                ◇ —
                ♣ K Q J 4
 ♠ K J 7 4
 ♡ J 10 9 8        N
 ◇ A 7 6 5     W       E
 ♣ A               S
```

'A diamond was, in fact, led,' said the Penguin. 'Declarer ruffed in dummy, crossed to his hand with the ♡ Q and played the ♠ 8. Do you cover?'

'I am not the Rabbit, you know,' retorted O.O. scornfully.

'Declarer runs the eight and it holds, East contributing the two. Now comes the ten of trumps. Again, do you cover?'

'I am still not the Rabbit,' repeated Oscar with a touch of irritation. 'But surely this fantasy did not happen in real life?'

'Happened roughly twenty minutes ago,' interjected the Hog, who had come over with the Corgi to join us. Stuffing half a dozen olives down his capacious gullet, H.H. gave the Penguin time to continue.

'East', proceeded P.P., 'followed to both spades and now declarer reeled off four diamonds, throwing clubs from dummy. On the fourth round East, too, discarded a club. A fifth diamond follows. Do you ruff?'

Oscar paused to consider. 'If you do,' went on P.P., 'declarer overruffs in dummy, draws your last trump, goes back to his hand with the king of hearts and leads his sixth diamond, squeezing you in hearts and clubs.'

'I don't ruff. I—er—throw a heart,' declared Oscar with conviction.

'Then', continued the Penguin, 'declarer discards dummy's last club, plays a heart to the ace, returns to the closed hand with the king, and again leads his sixth diamond. If you ruff, it will be the same mixture as before. Declarer will overruff, draw your remaining trump and make his thirteenth trick with a baby heart, which will now be master. If you don't ruff the last diamond, throwing instead your ♣ A, declarer, with two cards left, will lead a club through your K J of trumps up to the A Q on the table. Again it will be a case of 7 ♠ redoubled, duly made.'

'With an overtrick as it were,' chipped in the Corgi.

The Penguin filled in the other hands. This was the deal in full:

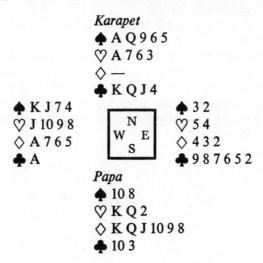

Karapet
♠ A Q 9 6 5
♡ A 7 6 3
◇ —
♣ K Q J 4

♠ K J 7 4   ♠ 3 2
♡ J 10 9 8   N   ♡ 5 4
◇ A 7 6 5   W E   ◇ 4 3 2
♣ A   S   ♣ 9 8 7 6 5 2

Papa
♠ 10 8
♡ K Q 2
◇ K Q J 10 9 8
♣ 10 3

'Who could have possibly landed in such an impossible contract?' expostulated O.O.

'Papa, of course,' replied the Hog, who had disposed of all the
olives in his immediate vicinity. 'It was the last board and he had
heard, as we all had, that there was a grand slam in spades about.
There had been no big spade hand before, so this had to be the
one. Well now,' went on H.H., raising a glass, 'put yourself in
Papa's place. You deal and pick up the South hand. What do you
do?'

Oscar opened his mouth.

'Wrong, as usual,' said H.H. severely, 'if you will only listen,
instead of interrupting, I'll tell you. Papa called 1 ♠ and rightly
so, mind you. It was a prepared bid. If the grand slam belonged
to the other side, the psychic 1 ♠ would put them off. If, on the
other hand, Karapet had solid spades and a few aces on the side,
they'd still get to 7 ♠, and what's more, Papa would play the
hand. So, you see, all in all, it was a perfectly good bid, if a trifle
unorthodox.'

'Orthodox or not, I am glad that Papa got at least one top,'
observed the Owl charitably. 'Things had not been going at all
well for him. Not his night out, by any means.'

'No, no, Papa got an average on the board,' said the Hog,
grimacing as he put down an empty glass. He hated people who
drowned their whisky in soda.

'An average for making 7 ♠ redoubled on that lot?' The Owl
could not believe it.

'It's simple enough,' explained H.H. 'Papa was right in assuming that it was the grand slam hand, but as you can see, the contract is absurd—with the cards as they are. Of course, 7 ♠ is
cold on the North-West hands and that's how it was until the
penultimate round when the Rabbit, who was South, replaced his
hand in the West slot.'

9. The Best Defence

'What a way to present a problem!' stormed the Hog, crumpling up in disgust Oscar's newspaper. 'South to make ten tricks against the best defence. And what sort of South, I should like to know, allows his opponents to put up the best defence?'

'Well . . .' began Oscar the Owl, our official kibitzer.

'On the contrary,' retorted the Hog warmly, 'East-West can only defend as well as South allows them to do. And if they put up the best defence it can only mean that South doesn't know his business. So why should anyone care how this ignoramus sets about making ten tricks?'

'But surely,' objected the Rueful Rabbit, 'that can't be right. I mean, when I'm East or West, I produce the worst defence no matter what South does, so it must work the other way, too. I mean. . . .'

The Hideous Hog wasn't listening. With bold strokes of my biro he was writing down a hand on the tablecloth.

♠ 7 5
♡ A 6 5
◇ K Q 10
♣ A K J 10 7

```
    N
 W     E
    S
```

♠ K 9 2
♡ J
◇ A J 9 4 3 2
♣ 8 4 3

West	North	East	South
1 ♠	Dble	Pass	3 ◇
Pass	4 ◇	Pass	5 ◇

'There you are,' said H.H., 'West opens a trump against 5 ◇.
Go ahead, Oscar.'

'I draw trumps and I *don't* take the club finesse,' announced the
Owl after due deliberation. 'If the finesse is right, I don't need it
for I don't mind giving up the lead to West. He can't hurt me.
But I want to keep East out, if possible, and I must give myself the
chance of finding him with a doubleton queen.'

'Well, he hasn't,' said H.H., beaming malevolently at the Owl.
'East's queen is fully protected and you may rest assured that
East—or any other nitwit, for that matter—will shoot a spade
through your gizzard the moment he gains the lead. Yes, you can
rely implicitly on the best defence.'

'If everything's wrong,' protested O.O., 'it would need a
magician to make this contract.'

The Hog cast down modestly his thick red eyelashes. 'I made it,
of course. Of course,' he repeated. 'But then I didn't allow East to
put up the best defence.'

'How did you do it?' inquired the Rueful Rabbit, all agog.

'Quite simple,' replied the Hideous Hog, snarling prettily, 'and
I'll show you how you, too, can do it.

'Suppose that the opening lead had not been a trump but a heart. The king to be precise. You would have ducked. Then you would have thrown a club on the ♡ A and you would have ruffed the third club, setting up two clubs in dummy—and you would have kept East at arm's length all the time.'

'Well, you do the same thing with a trump lead, because you expect West, on the bidding, to have the ♡ K. There's not much for him to have, anyway, but he's more likely to be missing a queen than a king. Now you see it all clearly, don't you?' asked the Hog, certain that no one could see anything.

His gaze swept round the table, but every glass was empty and with a dejected look he drained his own before continuing:

'At trick two you lead a heart from dummy. West takes your knave with the king, but he can't hurt you and you have all the time in the world to set up the clubs.'

'You are assuming that West has the ♡ K Q,' objected Oscar.

'Not at all,' replied the Hog. 'What's more he didn't. This was the deal:

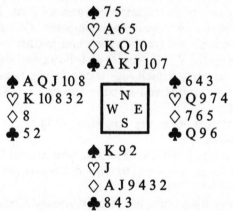

```
                    ♠ 7 5
                    ♡ A 6 5
                    ◇ K Q 10
                    ♣ A K J 10 7
   ♠ A Q J 10 8          N          ♠ 6 4 3
   ♡ K 10 8 3 2      W       E      ♡ Q 9 7 4
   ◇ 8                   S          ◇ 7 6 5
   ♣ 5 2                            ♣ Q 9 6
                    ♠ K 9 2
                    ♡ J
                    ◇ A J 9 4 3 2
                    ♣ 8 4 3
```

'Of course,' concluded H.H., 'East can break the contract by going up with the ♡ Q. But why should he do anything so eccentric? By taking into account that East is a rational human being and not a cardinal point, declarer makes his 5 ◇. And don't blame East either. The best defence doesn't call for clairvoyance.'

With a hearty tug at the tablecloth the Hog made room for another hand.

Back to Square One

Dealer North: N/S Vulnerable

♠ A J 10 9 8 7
♡ J
◇ Q 7 6
♣ A Q 10

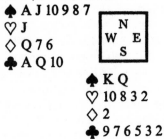

♠ K Q
♡ 10 8 3 2
◇ 2
♣ 9 7 6 5 3 2

North	East	South	West
Pass	4 ♡	ALL PASS	

'You are South,' said H.H. 'North, the dealer, passes. East opens 4 ♡ at favourable vulnerability and all pass. No catch, I promise you. Well, you open your singleton ◇ 2 and fortune smiles. The ◇ 6 is played from dummy and partner's knave wins, declarer dropping the ◇ 10. The ◇ K follows and declarer finds the ◇ 9. It's your turn. Which four tricks do you hope to make?'

'A couple of diamonds and a spade and er. . . .' The Rabbit's voice tailed off.

'North might just have the singleton ♡ Q. . . .' began the Emeritus Professor.

'In which case', pointed out the Hog, 'you cannot fail to make two trump tricks in addition to two diamonds, so there's no problem.'

'You cash *three* diamonds, not two,' suggested Colin the Corgi. 'If North had seven he would have probably opened 3 ◇ as dealer and if he has no more than six, declarer must have three.'

'And the fourth trick?' persisted the Hog, without taking his eyes off the cheese soufflé.

'That spade . . .' ventured the Penguin.

H. H. shook his head. 'Declarer cannot have fewer than six hearts for his bid and as Colin has rightly deduced, he should have three diamonds. That leaves four black cards at most, so if there's a spade loser, it will be thrown on a club. Declarer must surely have the king or North would not have passed originally.'

There was silence while the last of the Vosne Romanée slithered softly down the Hog's gullet. Then Oscar blinked twice in quick succession. Fearing that he had found the solution, H.H. hastened to give it.

'Since declarer must have at least three diamonds, you have to find *two* discards, not one. Does that suggest anything? No? Then I'll tell you. Throw both your spades. They are no good to you, anyway, since we've just seen that declarer can't have a spade loser. After taking his diamonds, partner will lead a spade and whether declarer ruffs or discards, you'll be certain of a trump trick.' As he spoke, H.H. filled in the deal.

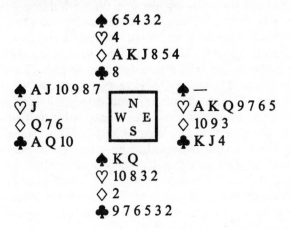

```
              ♠ 6 5 4 3 2
              ♡ 4
              ◇ A K J 8 5 4
              ♣ 8
♠ A J 10 9 8 7        ┌───────┐        ♠ —
♡ J                   │   N   │        ♡ A K Q 9 7 6 5
◇ Q 7 6               │ W   E │        ◇ 10 9 3
♣ A Q 10              │   S   │        ♣ K J 4
                      └───────┘
              ♠ K Q
              ♡ 10 8 3 2
              ◇ 2
              ♣ 9 7 6 5 3 2
```

'A pretty defence, H.H.,' said the Owl. 'Did you find it at the time or was it a happy afterthought?'

'I leave afterthoughts to others,' replied the Hog with some asperity, looking fixedly at the Professor. 'Of course, I would have found this defence. Unfortunately, I happened to be North and partner didn't think of it—or of anything else for that matter. He wasn't that sort. I had to leave it all to delcarer and though he did his best, there was no play for it. He just couldn't go down.'

'What happened?' asked O.O. He wasn't especially curious, but unless the Hog could be kept talking the chances of a second glass of Chateau Yquem would vanish for evermore.

'After taking three diamonds,' replied the Hog without letting go the bottle, 'I led my singleton club. Declarer was a true bridge technologist, the erudite type who always knows how to give himself that extra quarter per cent chance, but isn't quite so good with the 10–1 on propositions. He won the club on the table and ruffed a spade. It was an automatic reflex, you understand, just simple routine for an advanced technician, as he told us himself later. . . .'

'Yes, yes,' broke in the Rabbit eagerly. 'I know all about it. The ruff sets the stage for a trump coup in case North should have all five trumps. It's in my book. Chapter XXVIII.'

'That's just it,' said the Hog,' you all know so much about Chapter XXVIII these days that you forget about Chapter I. Look it up and see the odds against any player holding sixteen cards. That's what North would need for the trump coup to take effect—six diamonds, of which we know, five hearts and five black cards. Bah! Forget Chapter XXVIII and go back to square one. You'll do far better, all of you, if you don't try to play so well.

'Where was I?' asked the Hog two swallows later. 'Ah yes, square one. The shock of bringing down the king on the first round of spades cleared declarer's head a bit and he decided to draw trumps, just as any lesser non-technical mortal might do. Taking the knave was easy, but now he had to get back to his hand and he was too frightened to lead another spade. So he played a club, but alas I had no trump for it. The injustice of it! Partner could break the contract, but didn't. Declarer tried to lose it, but couldn't, and there was nothing left for me but to tell the other two what I thought of them.'

10. An Ode to the Deuce

'Of course, I hold better cards than you do,' declared the Hideous Hog after despatching his last helping of *Coq au Vin*. 'Since I win as many tricks with my kings as you people do with your aces, it stands to reason that I have more *de facto* aces than you, and more kings and queens, too, for that matter.'

We were dining at the Griffins with Oscar the Owl and the Rueful Rabbit, and the Hog was explaining to us why he was such an outstanding card-holder.

'Mind you,' he said, 'the high cards are purely incidental. Why, I've known even Papa take tricks with aces and kings—when he's in form, that is. The true mark of the virtuoso is the gift of enlisting on his side the lowly twos and threes and fours. Yes, my friends, if I had to write poetry,' went on H.H. raising my glass with a far-away look, 'I would compose an Ode to the Deuce, the greatest card in the pack.'

Picking up a handsome leather-bound volume which Oscar had brought with him, the Hog scribbled a hand on the fly leaf. 'Don't worry,' he told Oscar reassuringly, 'I shan't lose your place.'

F

Dealer South: E/W Vulnerable

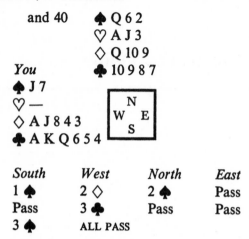

and 40   ♠ Q 6 2
           ♡ A J 3
           ◇ Q 10 9
You   ♣ 10 9 8 7
♠ J 7
♡ —
◇ A J 8 4 3
♣ A K Q 6 5 4

South	*West*	*North*	*East*
1 ♠	2 ◇	2 ♠	Pass
Pass	3 ♣	Pass	Pass
3 ♠	ALL PASS		

'You, West, lead the ♣ K,' went on H.H., 'and partner pro-
duces the knave. You continue with the ◇ A and he follows with
the ◇ 2. What's the next move?'

The Hog helped himself to *profiteroles au chocolat* and did not
speak again until he was down to the last three.

'Come, come,' he said, 'you've had plenty of time to select the
next card. Four tricks will hinge on it. Which is it to be?'

'The ♣ 6,' hazarded the Rueful Rabbit. 'Partner will wonder
why I didn't play the ace, guess the heart position, and after
ruffing the club, will lead a heart which I, in turn, will ruff.' The
Rabbit sat back contentedly, feeling that he had rarely talked
such good bridge in all his life.

'The only flaw in this pretty picture,' replied H.H. 'is that
partner can't have a singleton club. Don't forget the bidding. He
gave preference by passing 3 ♣ and with a singleton in both
minors he would have probably put you back to diamonds. But
even if you suspect him of failing in his duty, you must still play a
diamond. Think of that deuce. With a doubleton, partner would
have started a peter, and with three diamonds and one club he
would have definitely gone back to your first suit. Besides,' went
on H.H., 'a singleton club is no use to you, anyway, for you could
only get one heart ruff, while a singleton diamond is worth four

tricks—two diamond ruffs and two heart ruffs.' The Hog filled in the other hands:

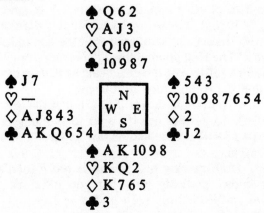

```
                    ♠ Q 6 2
                    ♡ A J 3
                    ◇ Q 10 9
                    ♣ 10 9 8 7
    ♠ J 7                          ♠ 5 4 3
    ♡ —            N               ♡ 10 9 8 7 6 5 4
    ◇ A J 8 4 3  W   E             ◇ 2
    ♣ A K Q 6 5 4  S               ♣ J 2
                    ♠ A K 10 9 8
                    ♡ K Q 2
                    ◇ K 7 6 5
                    ♣ 3
```

'That ◇ 2,' he said, 'should have given you the key. Petering with a singleton is a little unusual, perhaps, but there's nothing a deuce won't do for you if you treat it with kindness and understanding.'

Oscar made a half-hearted attempt to recover his book, but the Hog held on to it tightly as he wrote down this hand on the last page.

Dealer West: N/S Vulnerable

```
                    ♠ J 9 8
                    ♡ 4 3 2
                    ◇ A 3
                    ♣ A J 10 9 5   You
                               ♠ 7 6
                    N          ♡ J 10 9
                  W   E        ◇ K J 4 2
                    S          ♣ K 8 7 6
```

West	North	East	South
Pass	Pass	Pass	1 ♠
2 ◇	3 ♣	3 ◇	3 ♠
Pass	4 ♠	ALL PASS	

'This time you are East,' he told us. 'It's all quite straightforward. South opened 1 ♠, fourth in hand, and you supported partner's diamonds over North's 3 ♣. Now, against 4 ♠, partner reels off the ♡ Q, ♡ K and ♡ A before switching to a diamond. Declarer goes up with the ace and continues with the ace and a small club. Over to you.' The Hog pointed the nutcrackers straight at the Owl.

O.O. hooted softly. For the time being he had no other comment to make and the Rabbit took up the cue.

'I play low,' he ventured, 'for if South had the queen he would have finessed. So partner has it.' Next to shuffling, finessing was the best part of R.R's game and he saw no reason to hide his light under a bushel.

'No, no,' H.H. quickly brushed aside the Rabbit's reasoning. 'Declarer knows perfectly well that you have the ♣ K. Once again, think of the bidding. West passed as dealer, yet in addition to claiming some sort of diamond suit, he has produced the three top honours in hearts. He cannot have the ♣ K as well, so there's no point in a forlorn finesse and declarer's only hope is to put you to a guess, playing the clubs as he did.'

'But', went on the Hog, brandishing the nutcrackers belligerently, 'you haven't troubled to inquire what clubs fell on the ace. Just the same, I'll tell you. Declarer contributed the four and West the three.'

'But surely,' protested O.O., 'only the queen matters, the two, three and four being equals.'

'And *anyone* could have that deuce,' put in the Rabbit.

'Precisely,' agreed the Hog. 'But do you see the magic of that card? If declarer has it, he will follow suit on the second round, so East breaks the contract by going up with the king. And if West has the deuce, his three was clearly the beginning of a signal to show a doubleton. If so, declarer has the queen and once again East must play the king.'

The Rueful Rabbit was torn between admiration and suspicion. 'You worked it all out and went up with the king and broke the contract?' he asked twitching an eyebrow incredulously.

The Hideous Hog gave him a pitying look. 'I happened to be South,' he said, 'and, of course, I made the impossible contract. To an—er—card-holder such as myself it presented no great difficulty. These were the four hands.

♠ J 9 8
♡ 4 3 2
♢ A 3
♣ A J 10 9 5   *You*

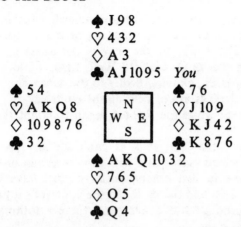

♠ 5 4   ♠ 7 6
♡ A K Q 8   ♡ J 10 9
♢ 10 9 8 7 6   ♢ K J 4 2
♣ 3 2   ♣ K 8 7 6

♠ A K Q 10 3 2
♡ 7 6 5
♢ Q 5
♣ Q 4

'East, you see,' explained H.H., 'took no more interest in dueces than you seem to do. Fearing that I might ruff out the clubs, he played low, allowing me to make my queen. After two rounds of trumps, ending on the table, I led the ♣ J and East lost his king—both his kings, I should say, for they vanished into thin air at the same time. I still had a trump entry on the table and could park my losing diamond on the set-up club—and all because East had failed to pay proper respect to a deuce.'

There were no more wide open spaces in Oscar's book and with a grunt H.H. allowed the Owl to remove it. On the back of the menu he wrote down:

♠ J 10
♡ J 2
♢ 4 3
♣ A Q J 10 6 5 4
            You
            ♠ 7 6 5 4
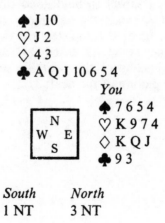
            ♡ K 9 7 4
            ♢ K Q J
            ♣ 9 3

South	North
1 NT	3 NT

'You are East, once more,' he announced. 'Nothing could be more straightforward than the bidding or more depressing than the dummy. The 1 NT, by the way is the usual 12–14 variety. Partner opens the ♠ Q. Got it? Well, then, while we pass the port,' went on H.H., clinging firmly to the decanter, 'you can tell me what our chances are of beating the contract.'

Oscar blinked, while the Rabbit began to count the dummy's clubs.

Two glasses later O.O. said: 'I can't see any problem here. Since partner's lead marks him with nine points in one suit and I have nine more in two others, declarer must have what's left, including two aces and the ♣ K. So the contract's icy cold unless partner can produce five spades and there's nothing I can do about it except hope.'

'But what do you want partner to do?' asked H.H.

'Double,' suggested the Rabbit.

'I want him to carry on with his spades, of course,' said O.O.

'Which card do you play then?' persisted the Hog.

'Oh, something midly encouraging, I suppose,' replied the Owl, 'the five or the six or the seven. It doesn't matter much, really, for my fourth spade is purely ornamental. If partner has four spades only, we are lost and if he has five, I don't need more than three.'

'Designate your card,' demanded the Hog.

'The one nearest my thumb,' retorted the Owl irritably.

'How can you expect to hold good cards,' cried the Hideous Hog indignantly, 'when they all look alike to you? And once again you have ignored completely the two and the three.'

'Where do they come in?' asked O.O. and R.R. in unison.

With vicious stabs of the Rabbit's slim gold pen, the Hog completed the picture of the deal:

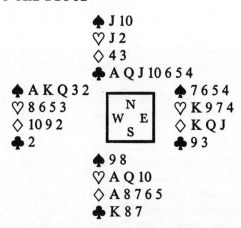

♠ J 10
♡ J 2
◇ 4 3
♣ A Q J 10 6 5 4

♠ A K Q 3 2   ♠ 7 6 5 4
♡ 8 6 5 3   ♡ K 9 7 4
◇ 10 9 2   ◇ K Q J
♣ 2   ♣ 9 3

♠ 9 8
♡ A Q 10
◇ A 8 7 6 5
♣ K 8 7

'Can you see it now?' he bellowed. 'Unless your thumb
happened to be resting nearest the seven, you will have done your
best to confuse partner and to block his suit. Didn't you say
yourself just now, and rightly so, for once, that you would encourage him to continue whether you had four spades or only
three? And if he sees you signal with the six, won't he think that
you are denying the seven?'

'Well . . .' began the Rabbit.

'Not well at all,' barked H.H. 'if West places declarer with the
seven, he must lead out his three tops to drop it. If you have four
to the seven, West must play two tops only, then the two to your
four or five, for otherwise the suit will be block. But if you make
no distinction between one small card and another, how can
partner know what to do?'

'So, you were East and you played the seven?' asked the Rabbit
looking sceptical.

'I was West and partner played the six,' replied H.H.

'And then?' inquited the Owl, raising the bushy eyebrows over
his round amber eyes.

'Partner echoed feebly with the five on my king and I underled
the ace. His seven won the third trick and my ace and three took
the next two.'

'Brilliant!' exlaimed R.R.

'A shrewd piece of guesswork,' agreed O.O.

'No guesswork at all,' chortled H.H. 'You should have seen

that precious professor of yours, the fellow with the long, thin legs who looks like a Secretary Bird. No sooner did he see dummy than he tore into the Walrus, who was his partner.'

'Twelve,' the Walrus had announced, taking three points for the long clubs.

'If instead of counting points, you'd bid your suit,' hissed S.B., 'we would be in a game which depended, at worst, on a finesse, instead of landing in this impossible contract.'

'Well now,' went on the Hideous Hog curving his lips in a warm, friendly sneer, 'he wouldn't have been so cross if he'd had a third spade, would he?' The suit might have broken 4–4 when all's said and done. So, you see, I wasn't fooled by that silly six.'

'A thoughtless card,' agreed the Owl.

'An absurd card,' echoed the Rabbit. 'It might have murdered your little deuce, the fifth, decisive trick for the defence. Who was this ridiculous partner. I mean. . . .'

'*You* were, last Wednesday,' broke in the Hog, passing politely the empty decanter to the Rueful Rabbit.

11: Papa Has the Last Word

'And what's wrong with gloating?' asked the Hideous Hog. Sipping a green Chartreuse, after a light meal of foie gras, lobster Thermidor, Chateaubriand à la Planche and crêpes Suzette, H.H. was in philosophic mood.

'This pious horror of gloating,' he mused aloud, 'springs from the lowest motives. The losers envy the winners and resent them. Yet what is gloating but a natural urge to savour fully a well-earned success, giving it added emphasis, perhaps, so as to share it with friends?

'Maybe, that as they say, I gloat more than others do,' went on the Hideous Hog, a benign glow spreading over his shiny pink countenance, 'but isn't that simply because I win more and am reluctant, being sociable by nature, to keep my little triumphs to myself? Is that a sin? When all is said and done,' pursued the Hog, 'the occasional jeer, the odd whoop or two, are only intended to bring out the finer points of the play, which might otherwise ⸱scape attention. 'No,' concluded the Hog, 'I see no virtue in false modesty. When I bring off a coup, I admit it fearlessly and frankly, and I do not care if all the world knows about it!'

Two hands that afternoon had given H.H. special pleasure and had prompted, no doubt his disquisition on the merits of gloating. Both occurred in the same rubber and found H.H., harnessed to the Rabbit, opposing Papa the Greek and the Emeritus Professor of Bio-Sophistry, known on account of his appearance as the Secretary Bird.

Papa made game on the first hand and dealt the next one. The Hideous Hog was sitting South.

Dealer West: E/W Vulnerable

```
        N
    W       E
        S
```

♠ A Q 10 4 3 2
♡ 6 5 4 3 2
♢ 3 2
♣ —

West	North	East	South
Papa	R.R.	S.B.	H.H.
1 ♡	Pass	3 ♢	Pass
4 ♢	Pass	4 ♡	Pass
4 ♠	Pass	5 ♣	Pass
5 NT	Pass	7 ♢	?

H.H. was in a quandary. Before invoking the grand slam force, Papa had cue-bid spades. Obviously that showed a void since the Hog himself had the ace. Therefore, Papa had a five (or six) card suit, presumably hearts. His partner had supported hearts and H.H. had five himself. That left none for R.R. and it followed that the defence could take a ruff at trick one and break the slam from the start. The prospect was pleasing, but wouldn't that Rabbit spoil everything by applying the Lightner double? It was inevitable. Already the Hog could see his partner's delicate nostrils atwitch with excitement and there could be little doubt, that once they were warned, opponents would quickly switch. The Secretary Bird might even bid 7 NT in the fond belief that Papa's cue-bid showed, not a void, but the ♠ A. Against 7 NT would it occur to the Rueful Rabbit to lead a spade? Most unlikely. The contract would doubtless be made and for months, if not for years, Papa would boast of having made a grand slam in no trumps at the Hog's expense with the entire spade suit out against him. It was not a pleasant thought.

If only opponents could be induced somehow to stay in 7 ♢, the one contract they could not possibly make. Could this be contrived? After a grunt or two, the Hog felt that he had the answer. He would double himself! Since it would be his own lead, no one would suspect an impending ruff and all would be well.

No sooner said than done. Alas, the Hog had reckoned without Papa. The double came as a relief to the Greek who had never cherished the prospect of whiling the time away as dummy for the benefit of S.B., who would have all the fun of wrapping up the grand slam. Now the double gave him a ready-made excuse for taking charge of the situation and he promptly bid 7 ♡.

After two passes, the Hideous Hog found himself tossed on the razor-edge horns of a new dilemma. A club lead would kill the grand slam in a matter of seconds and a spade would have the same effect a little later—unless, that is, Papa had started with six hearts. But wasn't the Rabbit just as likely to open a diamond as a club or a spade? The Hog decided that the risk was too great. The grand slam would cost 2410. The price of a sacrifice in 7 ♠ was unlikely to exceed 700 and might even be less.

With a martyred look, the Hideous Hog bid 7 ♠, all set to blame the Rueful Rabbit afterwards for having intended to lead a diamond against 7 ♡. These were the four hands.

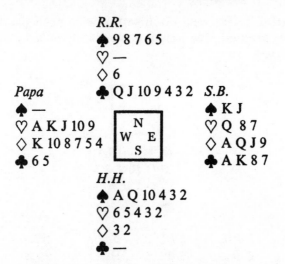

```
                      R.R.
                  ♠ 9 8 7 6 5
                  ♡ —
                  ◇ 6
    Papa          ♣ Q J 10 9 4 3 2   S.B.
♠ —                                  ♠ K J
♡ A K J 10 9        ┌─────────┐      ♡ Q 8 7
◇ K 10 8 7 5 4      │ W  N  E │      ◇ A Q J 9
♣ 6 5              │    S    │      ♣ A K 8 7
                    └─────────┘
                      H.H.
                  ♠ A Q 10 4 3 2
                  ♡ 6 5 4 3 2
                  ◇ 3 2
                  ♣ —
```

After the formality of a double, Papa opened the ♡ K which the Hog ruffed in dummy. The ♣ Q was covered by the ace and trumped in the closed hand. A second heart ruff was followed by the ♣ J from the table. S.B. played low and H.H. threw a diamond. The next club was covered and ruffed and a third heart was trumped in dummy. The defence was powerless. If S.B. did not ruff dummy's long clubs, the Hog would discard two hearts in the wake of his two losing diamonds and would remain on the table to take the trump finesse. So S.B. ruffed. The Hog overruffed, dropped the king of trumps and ruffed a fourth heart in dummy; thirteen tricks, made up of: six trumps in the closed hand; three of dummy's clubs—three were ruffed—and four heart ruffs.

While the Secretary Bird stamped and hissed, and Papa spluttered with impotent rage, the Rabbit apologized for not redoubling. 'I wasn't worried about the contract,' he explained, 'for I had a good deal more than I promised, but I didn't want to drive them into 7 NT. I mean, one never knows, does one? Both sides had bid spades, so it wasn't all that clear who had what or why and though, of course, I believe my partner, it's usually best to believe no one. I mean. . . .'

H.H. Speeds Things Up

The Rueful Rabbit went on dithering as he dealt the next hand, while the exultant Hog jeered, gloated and winked meaningly at the kibitzers.

```
              ┌─────────┐   ♠ 7 3
              │    N    │   ♡ K 7 6 5 2
              │  W   E  │   ◇ A K 4
              │    S    │   ♣ A K J
              └─────────┘
        ♠ 9 8
        ♡ Q 10 9
        ◇ Q J 10 6
        ♣ 10 8 5 2
```

North	East	South	West
R.R.	S.B.	H.H.	Papa
Pass	1 ♡	Pass	1 NT
Pass	2 NT	Pass	3 NT

After a pass from the Rabbit, the Secretary Bird opened 1 ♥ and a minute later Papa was declarer in 3 NT. The Rabbit opened the ♠ Q which was taken by Papa with the ace. A club to the table, won by the knave, came next and this was followed by the ♥ 2. The Hideous Hog looked round, noting with approval that he was still the centre of attention. The kibitzers had not forgotten that grand slam and all eyes were riveted upon him. Waving two cards demonstratively in mid-air, he let them fall simultaneously from his hand. As the ♥ Q and the ♠ 9 drifted to the table, the Hog announced: 'Two down', adding in a peremptory tone: 'Your deal, Professor.' The wild tufts of hair which project at right angles from the Secretary Bird's dome-shaped head, bristled in anger. 'Kindly explain,' he hissed, pulling at his satin tie of rich bilious yellow. Papa looked like a man trying to express inexpressible contempt and he was succeeding pretty well.

'You can see it, of course,' said the Hog grimacing to the kibitzers, 'but as they want me to dot the 'i's and cross the 't's, here goes. Since Papa is marked on the lead with the ♠ A K, he cannot have the ♥ A as well. That would be too much for his 1 NT response. So, my queen holds the trick and my spade clears partner's six-card suit while he still retains the ♥ A and. . . .'

'Who said that R.R. has six spades?' interposed Oscar the Owl.

'If he had only five,' replied the Hog with a superior smile, 'Papa would have four, and if so, he would have responded 1 ♠, not, 1 NT to the Professor's opening bid. And needless to say,' added H.H., 'if R.R. had seven spades he wouldn't have passed as dealer. Therefore he had precisely six, no more and no less.'

'But couldn't partner have a singleton ♥ A?' objected someone.

The Hog nodded sympathetically. 'You mean that even with four cards in partner's suit, Papa would have kept it dark so as to make sure of playing the hand himself? Yes, that's consistent with the bidding, but not with the play. With nine hearts between the two hands, he would have attacked the suit at once instead of using up one of his entries for the club finesse.'

This was the complete deal:

R.R.
♠ Q J 10 5 4 2
♡ A 4 3
◇ 7 5
♣ Q 4

Papa   S.B.
♠ A K 6   ♠ 7 3
♡ J 8   ♡ K 7 6 5 2
◇ 9 8 3 2   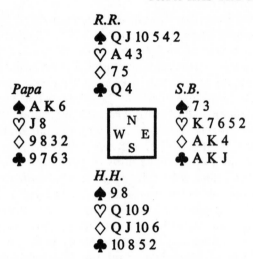   ◇ A K 4
♣ 9 7 6 3   ♣ A K J

H.H.
♠ 9 8
♡ Q 10 9
◇ Q J 10 6
♣ 10 8 5 2

The Hog turned to the Greek. 'Allow an old friend to give you a word of advice, Themistocles,' he said, pointing at Papa a fat pink forefinger. 'Winning the first trick with the ♠ A was unworthy of you. If you wanted to create doubt in my mind, the king was the corrrect card to play. The queen lead could be from, say, A Q J x x x, but not from K Q anything. Poor show, my friend. Who was it who made that witty remark about you—that you were so determined to false-card that you would do it even with a singleton? Ah, yes, I remember now, I said it myself. Ha! Ha!'

12. Co-operative Finesses

'Do you know,' said the Rueful Rabbit, looking pensively at an olive, 'I believe that the Hog thinks even less of Timothy as a player than he does of me.'

'Aren't you exag... er ... what makes you think so?' asked Oscar the Owl filling our glasses.

'Was he then so very rude to him this afternoon?' broke in Peregrine the Penguin, who had joined us in the bar. 'More so than usual, I mean?'

'That's just it', replied the Rabbit, 'he didn't scream at him once. Not a snort, not a jeer, not a word of abuse. Never have I known the Hog treat a partner with such studied contempt.'

I kibitzed throughout the afternoon session and I knew that Timothy the Toucan had felt deeply humiliated. Relations between H.H. and T.T. were friendly enough, at first, when they cut each other against Papa the Greek and Walter the Walrus.

'Shall we play co-operative doubles?' asked the Toucan, who had been reading up the subject. 'Certainly,' agreed the Hog. 'My doubles will be for penalties, yours for take-out. And don't save the rubber—that is, not this rubber.'

Walter the Walrus dealt and bid 1 NT. Sitting West, the Hog picked up:

♠ Q 4 3
♡ 4 3
◇ J 7 6 5
♣ A 8 5 2

North	East	South	West
W.W.	T.T.	Papa	H.H.
1 NT	Pass	3 ♡	Pass
4 ♡	Pass	4 ♠	Pass
5 ◇	Pass	5 ♡	Pass
6 ♡	ALL PASS		

After analysing the bidding sequence for fully five seconds, H.H. selected the ♣ 2 as his opening lead. The key to the auction, he told us later, was Papa's third round bid of 5 ♡. The trump suit had been agreed. He had cue-bid the ♠ A and the Walrus had shown the ◇ A. Why, then, was Papa willing to stop in 5 ♡? Clearly, because he had two club losers. And why did his partner bid the slam? Obviously, because he had the second round control in clubs. It was not a singleton, since he had opened 1 NT, so it must be the king. Therefore, explained the Hog, the best hope of breaking the slam was to find the Toucan, sitting over dummy's king, with the ♣ Q. If Papa had the ♣ J, in his own hand or in dummy, the unorthodox opening, away from the ace, would surely induce him to take the wrong view.

The Hog's diagnosis proved correct and these were, in fact, the four hands.

W.W.
♠ 10 2
♡ A Q 5
◇ A 10 9 8
♣ K 10 7 6

H.H.
♠ Q 4 3
♡ 4 3
◇ J 7 6 5
♣ A 8 5 2

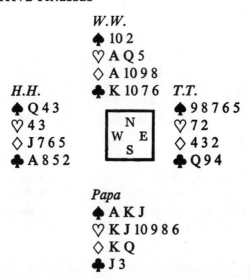

T.T.
♠ 9 8 7 6 5
♡ 7 2
◇ 4 3 2
♣ Q 9 4

Papa
♠ A K J
♡ K J 10 9 8 6
◇ K Q
♣ J 3

On the Hog's ♣ 2, Papa played low from dummy. The Toucan, after bouncing once or twice in his chair, his long shiny nose aglow with concentration, contributed the nine. Winning with the knave, much to his surprise, the Greek claimed all thirteen tricks.

'How could we have got there?' asked Walter the Walrus anxiously. 'Do you think that with 14 points and three tens I was too strong to open 1 NT?'

'Wasn't it right to finesse against dummy?' asked the Toucan. Some sixth sense told him that all was not well.

'A co-operative finesse, so to speak,' murmured Colin the Corgi, who had watched the play.

Papa chuckled contentedly. 'Such a pretty lead of yours,' he told H.H., 'and anyone—well almost anyone—would have played as Timothy did. Just goes to show, though, that two rights sometimes make a wrong. Ha! Ha!'

The Hog bared his teeth and glared, but he was snarling at the Greek, not at the Toucan, and Timothy knew in his heart of hearts that he had been found unworthy of so much as a passing insult.

Knockout Before Uppercut

The next hand was thrown in. Then Papa dealt and called 1 ♡.

G

♠ K Q J 10
♡ J 9 5
◇ 9 7 6 5
♣ Q J

♠ 8 7 5 3
♡ Q 2
◇ K Q J 3 2
♣ 3 2

```
        N
    W       E
        S
```

South	West	North	East
Papa	H.H.	W.W.	T.T.
1 ♡	Pass	1 ♠	2 ♣
3 ♡	Pass	4 ♡	

The Hideous Hog opened the ♣ 3. The Toucan went up with the ace and as Papa followed with the four, he turned to the ceiling for inspiration. Was the Hog's three a singleton? He could not tell and to reconnoitre the position he led the ◇ A. The Hog signalled violently with the king and when the ten followed, he overtook it with the knave to play the key card for the defence, the ◇ 2. These were the four hands:

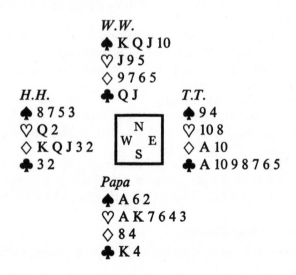

W.W.
♠ K Q J 10
♡ J 9 5
◇ 9 7 6 5
♣ Q J

H.H.
♠ 8 7 5 3
♡ Q 2
◇ K Q J 3 2
♣ 3 2

T.T.
♠ 9 4
♡ 10 8
◇ A 10
♣ A 10 9 8 7 6 5

Papa
♠ A 6 2
♡ A K 7 6 4 3
◇ 8 4
♣ K 4

It was some time before a startled Toucan, dazed and dazzled by his partner's eccentric diamond sequence, produced the ten of trumps, forcing the Greek's king and ensuring for the defence a fourth, decisive trick—the Hog's queen of trumps.

'The nine being in dummy, the eight would have done as well as the ten, Timothy,' pointed out the Rabbit. 'Not that it matters, of course, but well, you know, I mean. . . .'

'After what happened on the last hand,' retorted T.T. 'you won't catch me finessing against dummy again—whether it matters or not.'

In a loud aside to the kibitzers, the Hideous Hog paid a brief tribute to his defence. It had been clear to him from trick two, he explained, that only an uppercut could break the contract. The Toucan having shown up with two aces, Papa was marked with the other two and he could hardly have jumped to 3 ♡ without a six-card suit headed by the two top honours. The only hope was to find T.T. with the ten and to get him to play it. Could it be done? That was the burning question and the pyrotechnic display in diamonds was the answer. 'He did the right thing,' declared the Hog proudly, 'I shall never play better than that.'

'To uppercut declarer, first knock out partner,' observed Colin the Corgi.

13. The Art of Divination

'I confess,' admitted the Hideous Hog modestly, 'that I sometimes do the right thing for the wrong reason. Not making mistakes has become so much a habit, you see, that I don't always know myself how I do it. But have you observed,' he went on, 'how lesser players are spurred on to the lowest bids and plays by the loftiest motives? If only they knew less about the game they would not so often play so badly.'

We were discussing a hand on which the Hog's role had been confined to watching—or rather to sneering and jeering. His only interest at the Club—and away from it, too, no doubt—was to play and he found it insufferable to be kept waiting. He resented more especially slams and sacrifices. 'In *my* time,' he would say bitterly, 'spinning out the rubber to no purpose. Sheer undiluted selfishness. Typical of our age.'

Such was his mood when he sat down with me behind Papa, hopefully expecting the worst—that is, the worst for Papa, who picked up:

♠ K Q 10
♡ Q J
◇ K 10 6 5
♣ A Q 10 3

The Rueful Rabbit, who dealt sitting East, opened 3 ♠. South, the Emeritus Professor of Bio-Sophistry, looking more than ever like a Secretary Bird, called 3 NT, conventionally, for a take-out, and Timothy the Toucan, West, passed. It was quite apparent from the look of disdain on the Hog's face that Papa, sitting North, was predestined to do the wrong thing. The Greek, justly proud of his hand, looked for his part, more than a match for destiny. His first move was a cue-bid in opponents' suit—4 ♠ The Professor responded 5 ◇ and this Papa raised confidently to 6 ◇. The sequence had been:

West	North	East	South
T.T.	Papa	R.R.	S.B.
		3 ♠	3 NT
Pass	4 ♠	Pass	5 ◇
Pass	6 ◇		

'It would serve him right,' muttered the Hog, 'if that Toucan held a singleton spade and found his partner with the ace, just waiting to give him a ruff. Quite likely, too, on the bidding.'

Craning his short, thick red neck, to peer into Timothy's cards, H.H. swung back beaming with pleasure. 'There's some justice left in the world after all,' he whispered to me. Timothy the Toucan did, in fact, have a singleton spade. We turned to look over the Rabbit's shoulder and the Hog, digging me in the ribs, rubbed his podgy hands with glee. Without a doubt the Rabbit had been dealt the ♠ A and the stage was well and truly set for Papa's downfall. This was the deal.

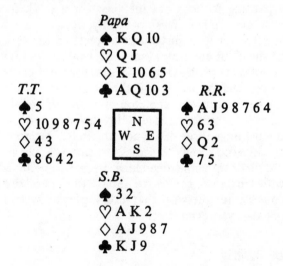

Papa
♠ K Q 10
♡ Q J
◇ K 10 6 5
♣ A Q 10 3

T.T.
♠ 5
♡ 10 9 8 7 5 4
◇ 4 3
♣ 8 6 4 2

R.R.
♠ A J 9 8 7 6 4
♡ 6 3
◇ Q 2
♣ 7 5

S.B.
♠ 3 2
♡ A K 2
◇ A J 9 8 7
♣ K J 9

After communing earnestly with the ceiling, the Toucan pro-

duced the ♡ 10. He explained afterwards that a spade lead could
serve no purpose since Papa's cue-bid of 4 ♠ had announced the
first round control. It was just possible, however, since he had
six or seven hearts himself that the Rabbit might have a void.

The Secretary Bird won the first trick in dummy and continued
with a trump to his ace. Everything depended on finding the
queen and since R.R., was marked with length in spades, S.B.,
decided to finesse against Timothy. The odds were with him, but
the finesse failed and the ♠ A sealed his fate.

A loud guffaw from the Hideous Hog cut him short before he
could begin to explain how unlucky he had been.

'What a silly contract!' cried H.H. 'A ruff on the opening lead
stands out a mile. A miracle saves him, yet he still manages to go
down. And all the time 6 NT is unbeatable.'

'Only on a guess,' protested the Emeritus Professor.

'No one but a moron . . . er present company excepted, I
suppose,' retorted the Hog courteously, 'could succeed in mis-
guessing the ◇ Q.'

Papa glared. The Secretary Bird hissed. The kibitzers flapped
their ears interrogatively, but no one put the obvious question, for
all knew that the Hog would answer it without being asked.

Barely pausing to hold out his glass for a refill, the Hog explained: 'Against 6 NT West probably opens a spade. If not,
declarer does it for him, just to get a count on the suit. Then, he
sets about the clubs and notes that East, who shows up with seven
spades, follows twice, leaving room for four red cards. All that
remains is for declarer to play his three top hearts. If East follows
all the way he must have a singleton diamond. If he follows twice,
he must have a doubleton and if he turns up with a singleton
heart, he must have three diamonds precisely. Declarer, of course
plays the suit accordingly. Needless to say, it's just as simple if
the Rabbit turns up with three clubs. In fact,' concluded the Hog
with a withering look round the table, 'the art of divination at
bridge consists in guessing that every player in turn is dealt
thirteen cards—yes, even R.R.'

Pragmatic Bidding

A dozen game hands later the Toucan and the Rabbit clinched the rubber. Timothy cut out and the Hog faced the Rabbit who dealt the first hand.

I was sitting between Papa and R.R. The Secretary Bird was East.

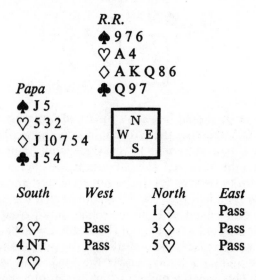

	R.R.	
	♠ 9 7 6	
	♡ A 4	
	◇ A K Q 8 6	
Papa	♣ Q 9 7	
♠ J 5		
♡ 5 3 2		
◇ J 10 7 5 4		
♣ J 5 4		

South	West	North	East
		1 ◇	Pass
2 ♡	Pass	3 ◇	Pass
4 NT	Pass	5 ♡	Pass
7 ♡			

The Greek opened the ◇ J, which brought the ace from dummy, the three from his partner and the two from declarer. Six hearts followed in quick succession. On the third round S.B. threw a low club and Papa began to count. He could see that by the time the Hog ran out of trumps six cards would be left. What should he keep? It was obvious from the bidding that H.H. had both black aces, but he could not have the ♣ K, too, for that would give him thirteen top tricks. Therefore, to protect his partner's king—in case declarer had A 10—Papa had to keep the knave and another club. Three diamonds were needed to look after the suit in dummy and that left room for one spade.

The position was clear enough and it only remained for Papa to decide the order of his discards. To give away as little as possible he cleverly left to the end the least important of his cards, the fifth, redundant diamond.

I strolled round the table to see how things looked from S.B.'s angle.

Dummy
♠ 9 7 6
♡ A 4
◇ A K Q 8 6
♣ Q 9 7   *S.B.*
                   ♠ Q 10 8
                   ♡ 7 6
   ┌─────────┐   ◇ 9 3
   │   N   │   ♣ K 10 8 6 3 2
   │ W   E │
   │   S   │
   └─────────┘

Which six cards should he keep? First and foremost he had to
retain the ◇ 9. Otherwise the Hog could take the marked finesse
against Papa's ten. He could let go three clubs, but not four,
since H.H. might have A J x. That meant, of course, that S.B.
would be down to two spades. It did not seem particularly important for if the Hog had the A K J, he could catch the queen anyway. On the other hand, if Papa, who had only parted with one
spade, had the king or knave, he could look after the suit on his own.

Somehow all the pieces did not fit into the puzzle and to get a
better understanding I joined Oscar the Owl, who was sitting
behind H.H. This was the picture which came into view.

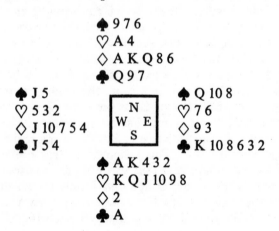

The Hog's last six cards were the ♣ A and the ♠ A K 4 3 2,
and by this time, all were winners.

'Why didn't you throw a diamond earlier to give me a count on the suit?' cried S.B. 'I could have discarded my nine and kept a third spade.'

While Papa spluttered with rage, Timothy the Toucan, who liked to see fair play, bounced uneasily in his chair. 'Don't you think' he ventured diffidently, 'that it was a little hard for Mr. Papadopoulos to guess that H.H., usually such a thoughtful player, had forgotten to cash his top diamonds while he had the chance. I mean er. . . .'

'What vile bidding,' broke in Papa who was beginning to regain the power of speech. 'How can one read correctly the hand of an illiterate? Why, he might have found four spades to the queen-knave in dummy and still the contract would have been 7 ♡. And yet some people think that he's the second best player in the club!'

'Do not fret, dear Papa,' gloated the Hideous Hog, 'my pragmatic bidding sequence would have proved too much even for an expert. A lesser player', went on H.H., bowing politely to the Greek, 'would have insisted on showing both majors. And why? Because for generations textbook addicts have been casting powerful two-suiters before sw . . . before—er—partners. Even now you don't seem to see that if the hand is good for 7 ♠, 7 ♡ must be there, too, though the reverse need not necessarily apply, as in this case. And that is why', concluded the Hog, deftly emptying the Toucan's glass, 'it is better to know too little about the game than too much. The result is, perhaps, the same, but it is less humiliating.'

Having to cut the pack for the next deal gave H.H. a tactical advantage. He exploited it by holding up proceedings for his peroration.

'The cost of good bidding,' he declared holding half the pack suspended in mid-air, 'can be prohibitive if it leads to a killing defence. Conversely, no bid is truly bad if it provokes a defence that is even worse.'

14. The Latest in Safety Plays

'Have you heard of any new safety plays lately?' asked the Rueful Rabbit eagerly as I walked into the bar at the Griffins.

The Rabbit was sipping a glass of Madeira after a particularly happy session. He had played well and knew it, and the Hog knew it, too, for apart from the usual epithets he had hardly insulted him half a dozen times all afternoon.

Twice in one rubber R.R. had brought off superlative safety plays and that meant a great deal to him for he had been reading up the subject assiduously and had learned whole pages by heart.

'Everyone of us,' he explained to me, 'has an individual style. Take the Hog, for example. You must have noticed that he holds longer suits than others do and he just loves to reel off sixes and sevens and fours and threes and things until everyone's pips rattle. That's what makes him so good at squeezing. I ought to know. I have been there all too often at the receiving end, feeling outnumbered on every deal.

'Or take Papa,' pursued the Rabbit swallowing another thimbleful of Madeira. 'A brilliant psychologist, who always knows what everyone will do, except that the Hog usually does something else.

'Now in my own case,' went on R.R., nibbling at an olive, 'my style is well suited to safety plays. I mean, the whole art lies in losing that extra trick, doesn't it? Well, it comes to me quite naturally. I mean. . . .'

This was one of the hands which gave R.R. the chance that afternoon to exercise his natural gifts—and his newly acquired book knowledge. He had cut the Hideous Hog against S.B., the Emeritus Professor of Bio-Sophistry, and Karapet Djoulikyan, the Free Armenian.

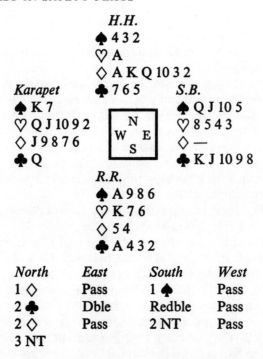

H.H.
♠ 4 3 2
♡ A
♢ A K Q 10 3 2
♣ 7 6 5

Karapet
♠ K 7
♡ Q J 10 9 2
♢ J 9 8 7 6
♣ Q

S.B.
♠ Q J 10 5
♡ 8 5 4 3
♢ —
♣ K J 10 9 8

R.R.
♠ A 9 8 6
♡ K 7 6
♢ 5 4
♣ A 4 3 2

North	East	South	West
1 ♢	Pass	1 ♠	Pass
2 ♣	Dble	Redble	Pass
2 ♢	Pass	2 NT	Pass
3 NT			

The bidding was straightforward. The Hideous Hog dealt and
opened 1 ♢. Over the Rabbit's response of 1 ♠ he made the
routine rebid of 2 ♣, that being one of the suits he did not want
led against him in no trumps. The Secretary Bird doubled to show
his disdain and the Rueful Rabbit redoubled as a gesture of
solidarity.

The Hog's rapid retreat into 2 ♢ put the Rabbit in a quandary.
He was too good to pass. He had no more suits to show and he
was not allowed to call no trumps, except in an emergency, in case
it led to his playing the hand. Still, this was an exceptional
situation, and in any case, it was hardly likely that the Hog would
let him be declarer.

The Hog's raise to 3 NT took everyone aback. Later, H.H. explained that it was psychic. A contract of 2 NT, with R.R. in
charge, might be doubled. But it could never dawn on anyone
that he would raise the Rabbit, voluntarily, without at least ten
stone-cold tricks.

Karapet, looking like a man who always expected the worst in life and whose expectations invariably came to pass, led the ♡ Q. His long, melancholy nose seemed longer and even more melancholy than usual.

The Rabbit began to count his tricks and there was joy in his heart, for stretching invitingly before him he could see a beautiful safety play, just like the ones in his book. To make his contract he needed no more than five of dummy's six diamond tricks and he could afford to give up the sixth if he could thereby make certain of the other five. A classical situation. All he had to do was to finesse the ten, losing perhaps to a singleton knave, but ensuring nine tricks for his contract.

'Page 133,' he said, thinking aloud, and nodding to himself gravely, he led the ◇ 4 towards the table.

'Stop!' hissed the Secretary Bird. 'The lead is in dummy.'

The Rueful Rabbit gurgled in exasperation. He was particularly anxious to finesse the ten, hoping to lose the trick to a singleton knave. Now, through sheer carelessness, he had missed the chance and it was very vexing. Of course, he could lose some other diamond, but it was not at all the same thing. Petulantly, he led dummy's ◇ 2. The Secretary Bird showed out and a few minutes later, when he had grasped the implications, the Rabbit brightened visibly, for fate had presented him with another opportunity to finesse the ten. The contract was now unbeatable.

'Why do you persecute me like this?' cried the Armenian with an anguished look at the Secretary Bird. 'Had you let him play peacefully from his hand he would have made four tricks only in diamonds and nothing could have saved him. By insisting wantonly on the letter of the law you found for him the perfect safety-play. You are a lawyer, Professor, yes, that's what you are.'

'No, no,' protested the Rabbit, feeling that Karapet had gone too far, 'I was going to finesse the ten anyway, so you see, it made no difference. I mean it's on page 133, except that the long suit is clubs, not diamonds. . . .'

Karapet was not listening. 'Why, oh why,' he murmured, 'does everything happen to *me*? Never would he have thought of a 5–0 distribution. Perhaps it is not even in his book.'

Ultra Virus

'Two more hands,' announced Timothy the Toucan, taking out his watch. 'I was only kibitzing to make you up, but I have an important dinner engagement.'

At game all and 60 to East-West the Rabbit found himself once more at the wheel in a game contract.

H.H.
♠ Q J 3 2
♡ K 9 2
◇ Q 9 8
♣ 10 3 2

```
      N
   W     E
      S
```

R.R.
♠ 5 4
♡ A J 8 3
◇ A K J 10
♣ A 9 4

South	West	North	East
1 ♡	1 ♠	1 NT	Pass
2 NT	3 ♣	3 ♡	Pass
4 ♡	Pass	Pass	Pass

Karapet (West) led the ♠ K and ♠ A, S.B. following with the ten and seven. Next came a low club to the Secretary Bird's king, which the Rueful Rabbit won with the ace. A quick glance at dummy, another at his own hand, and R.R. could identify seven tricks in the side-suits, leaving three more to be extracted from trumps for his contract. And was not there a safety play for precisely that situation on page 146?

'Goodnight,' said T.T. interrupting his train of thought. 'My dinner engagement is at seven and it is now seven-thirty. I shall be late if I don't go soon.'

'Wait for me,' pleaded the Rabbit. 'We shall be up after this hand and. . . .'

S.B. was there in a flash. 'That constitutes a claim under section 70,' he declared. Here was a chance to make up for his earlier *faux pas* and he was determined to make the most of it. 'Will you kindly make. . . .'

'. . . a comprehensive statement,' interrupted the Rabbit to complete the sentence. He had broken more rules than were dreamt of in S.B's philosophy and he knew the penalties by heart.

'Which tricks are you claiming?' inquired the Secretary Bird with a menacing gleam in his pince-nez.

'Four diamonds, the ♣ A, two spades and three trumps. Oh, yes,' explained R.R., 'there is a safety play. It's on page 146. You can make absolutely certain of three tricks.'

'How?' persisted S.B.

'The safety play', replied the Rabbit, 'is not to play the suit at all. Sooner or later someone else will have to do it.'

'Three down at least,' whispered Oscar the Owl, 'he's got two more clubs to lose and the Professor has six trumps.'

'Since you do not propose to draw trumps,' went on the inexorable Secretary Bird, 'you can hardly count two spade tricks. Pray be good enough to play.'

The Hideous Hog, who had remained strangely silent throughout the cross-examination, suddenly came to life.

'The Professor is quite right,' he said softly. Everyone looked up in alarm. 'Yes,' went on H.H., in his best Pecksniffian manner. 'You must not play spades.'

S.B. hissed loudly, but before he could formulate an objection, the Hideous Hog put up imperiously a fat, podgy pink hand. He did not wish to be interrupted.

'As the Professor was about to say,' went on H.H., 'you are obliged by the rules to follow your statement, card by card. In any case, I could not, for my part, accept any favour or concession. You must, I greatly fear, play the cards in the order announced by you—first the diamonds, then a club and finally the spades for, of course, you may not draw trumps. There is nothing for it, my dear R.R., you must pay for your little slip. The Professor is absolutely right.'

The Secretary Bird's hissing turned into a piercing whistle. Clearly that Hog was up to something, but on the spur of the moment S.B. could find no grounds for disagreeing with himself and the Rabbit was allowed to play on.

First he led out his four diamonds, discarding a club from dummy. S.B. followed all the way, but Karapet, who had two diamonds only, threw a club, then a spade. Next the Rabbit led a club. The Armenian went up with the queen, but the Professor ruffed his partner's trick and played the five of hearts. He could not help himself, for this was the deal.

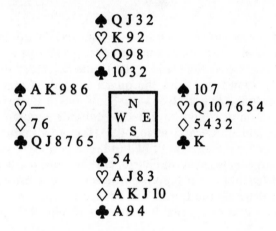

The Rabbit won the trick with the nine in dummy, and being forbidden to touch trumps, led a spade. S.B. ruffed and the Rabbit overruffed leaving this position.

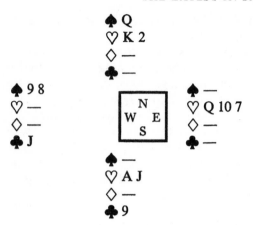

♠ Q
♡ K 2
◇ —
♣ —

♠ 9 8
♡ —
◇ —
♣ J

N
W E
S

♠ —
♡ Q 10 7
◇ —
♣ —

♠ —
♡ A J
◇ —
♣ 9

The ♣ 9 was ruffed with dummy's king and the queen of spades took effectively the finesse against the Professor's queen of trumps.

Frowning, Oscar the Owl turned to the Secretary Bird. 'Why,' he asked, 'didn't you lead the queen instead of a small trump when you ruffed that club? Deprived of one of his two entries to dummy, declarer would have had to concede a trump trick.'

'Come, come, Oscar,' jeered the Hog good-naturedly, 'you know these legal chaps don't like to break contracts—unless they are in charge themselves, of course. Ha! ha! Besides, who has ever heard of leading an unsupported queen from a broken six-card suit? What would the Lord Chief Justice say? Ultra Virus, I bet.'

'Is that a new safety play?' asked the Rueful Rabbit excitedly.

15: Too Much Psychology

As I walked into the bar at Griffins, the Hideous Hog was holding forth: 'Winning against good players calls for skill. Winning against bad ones is primarily a test of character.'

The Hog was seeking to enlighten Oscar the Owl, our Senior Kibitzer, who could not understand why superior technique at bridge brought such meagre rewards. Papa's was the case he had especially in mind.

'He lacks psychology,' said Peregrine the Penguin.

'He has too much psychology,' retorted H.H. 'That Greek is always trying to divine what other people are thinking, when most of the time they are incapable of any thought at all. Patience is the sharpest weapon against poor players. I don't mean that partners, or any other fools for that matter, should be suffered gladly. Far from it. But one must learn to sit back passively while opponents throw away unbreakable contracts and give away unmakeable ones. Of course, they may be given, here and there, a friendly push down the slippery slope, but generally speaking, they should be allowed to commit *felo de se* their own way.'

As he wrote down a hand on the back of a letter, which someone had asked him to post, H.H. added sententiously: 'To each according to his limitations, from each according to his disability.'

We looked at the hand.

H

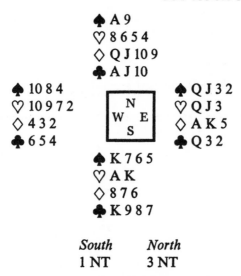

♠ A 9
♡ 8 6 5 4
◇ Q J 10 9
♣ A J 10

♠ 10 8 4
♡ 10 9 7 2
◇ 4 3 2
♣ 6 5 4

♠ Q J 3 2
♡ Q J 3
◇ A K 5
♣ Q 3 2

♠ K 7 6 5
♡ A K
◇ 8 7 6
♣ K 9 8 7

South	North
1 NT	3 NT

'You are East,' said H.H., 'the Walrus, who is your partner, opens the ♡ 2. Declarer takes your knave with the king and leads a diamond. You win and lead the ♡ Q, which falls to the ace. Another diamond and you are in again. Well, seeing all four hands, how do you propose to beat the contract?'

'Who is declarer?' asked Peregrine the Penguin cautiously.

'Another Walrus,' replied the Hog contemptuously. 'Different name, I believe, but just about as intelligent.'

While the Hog emptied a nearby whisky and a sherry, we pondered.

Routine Brilliance

'Elementary,' resumed H.H., returning Oscar's glass. 'Classical situation for switching to a spade. Routine piece of brilliance performed for the first time every year by at least a dozen masters. Since you don't lead a heart, South thinks you haven't got one and takes a club finesse the wrong way. You grab the queen, shoot the concealed heart across the table and declarer goes up in smoke.'

'And that's what you did?' asked Oscar the Owl.

'No,' replied the Hog with a crafty look, 'but then, you see, I

didn't have the ♣ Q. Ha! ha! Forgive my little deception and
now try again without the queen.'
   We must have looked suitably nonplussed for H.H. went
straight to the point. 'Against the particular South I've described,
there's nothing you can do. Just sit back, hoping that he mis-
guesses. He shouldn't, of course, for the ♣ Q would give you a
13 count and leave the Walrus with only 1. But then that type of
declarer is usually too busy counting his own points to notice
anyone else's. However,' continued H.H., looking crafty again, 'I
fear that I've misled you. To demonstrate my point I told you a
small white lie about South. Declarer was our old friend, the
Secretary Bird. . . .'
   'He notices everything,' interjected P.P., 'he has a quick, well-
trained legal mind.'
   'Exactly,' agreed the Hog, 'a pedant to his fingertips. So what
do you play?'
   Oscar side-stepped the question by ordering a round of drinks.
   'Against S.B.,' went on H.H., 'you play back your third heart
and on the next one you throw, nonchalantly, a little club. If you
are lucky, he will give you a dirty look. Of course, he knows that
you know that the club position is decisive. Why then, should you
discard one? To fool him, naturally. So you must have the
queen. . . .
   'That's what I was telling you, Oscar. When the numbskull's in
charge, you must sit back patiently allowing him to bring about
his own destruction. But the Secretary Bird is just good enough to
be given a friendly push.'
   'And did he slip?' asked the Penguin.
   'He would have done, undoubtedly,' replied H.H., with a sly
self-satisfied expression, which was as near as he could get to
looking benign. 'But, I must confess to you that S.B. wasn't the
declarer. I brought him in as an example of the type who deserved
a little subtlety, but on whom too much would be wasted. As it
happens, declarer was Papa, a far better player than S.B., but
desperately clever, as you know. Now what do you do?'
   'You didn't have the ♣ Q and Walter the Walrus was your
partner?' asked the Owl, who was growing suspicious.
   H.H. was dealing with too many olives to say anything, but he
nodded affirmatively.

'And you want Papa to think that you have the queen?' persisted Oscar.

The Hog nodded once more and turning over the letter, wrote down the North and East hands again in small characters under the air mail label. This time there was no queen of clubs.

♠ A 9
♡ 8 6 5 4
♢ Q J 10 9
♣ A J 10

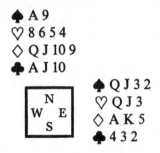

♠ Q J 3 2
♡ Q J 3
♢ A K 5
♣ 4 3 2

'Since you have clearly no idea,' said the Hog, 'I'll tell you. Go back to square one. After coming in with your ♢ A, that is the second time you are in, you *don't* return your small heart. Lead a spade.'

'The same play as the first time, when you had the queen and declarer was another Walrus?'

'Precisely,' agreed the Hog. 'And observe that Papa knows about that concealed heart. He must do, for the Walrus, the real one, opened the ♡ 2 and he is a well brought up nitwit, who always leads his fourth highest. He probably thinks it's immoral to do otherwise, like not counting his points or being rude to another man's wife. Now Papa spotted my piece of deception at once, as he was intended to do, and he assumed that I was luring him into a club finesse against the Walrus. So, of course, I must have the queen. Why, you could hear his blood tingle when he had worked it all out. Now you see what I mean, Peregrine, when I say that poor Papa has too much psychology?'

I remembered the hand and Walter's look of surprise when he came in with the ♣ Q. 'Never thought I'd get in to make those hearts,' he said, 'I only had 3 points, you know.'

Double Dummy Defence

'Another ten minutes for the *tournedos Rossini*,' announced M.

Merle. That gave us time for one more drink and while he waited politely for someone to order it, the Hideous Hog wrote down another hand.

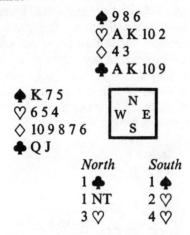

♠ 9 8 6
♡ A K 10 2
◇ 4 3
♣ A K 10 9

♠ K 7 5
♡ 6 5 4
◇ 10 9 8 7 6
♣ Q J

	North	South
	1 ♣	1 ♠
	1 NT	2 ♡
	3 ♡	4 ♡

'This time, there's no mystification,' said the Hog. 'Papa was declarer and I was West. I opened the ◇ 10 and found partner with the king and ace, declarer following with the queen and knave. Next came the ♠ 10, covered by the queen and taken by me with the king. Three tricks in the bag. Where do we find another?'

Before anyone could speak, H.H., was once more in full flood. 'Defend as I always do, that is, double dummy. If Papa has five spades there's no hope, for then he has only a doubleton club. But if he has two four-card majors, he must have three clubs and not knowing that my ♣ Q J are bare, he must think that he has a loser in the suit. Does that suggest anything? No? Very well, I'll tell you. The only hope is a trump trick. Now partner is most unlikely to have the queen, but he might just turn up with the knave, and if so, you must try to protect it.'

'Protect?' asked Oscar incredulously.

'In a manner of speaking,' pursued the Hog. 'To the fourth trick I led the ◇ 9 conceding a ruff and discard. Papa looked at me with intense suspicion. Why was I being so kind to him, allowing him to ruff in dummy and so get rid of his losing club? Could it be that I had taken a sudden liking to him? He thought there must be some other reason,' said H.H., chuckling. 'Well, what could it be? Work it out yourselves.'

Two or three gulps later, the Hog told us himself.

'Papa thought, as he was intended to think, that I was trying to protect my J x x x of trumps—to make him ruff in dummy so as to prevent him testing the trumps, seeing East show out and finessing against my knave. Having discovered my secret plan, he duly did as he was asked. First, he played dummy's king of trumps, then he came to his hand with a spade and then, in triumph, he finessed the heart. Partner was so surprised to make his ♡ J that he nearly revoked. These were the four hands.

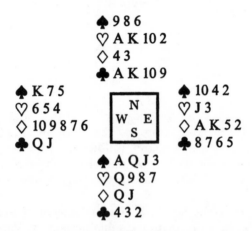

♠ 9 8 6
♡ A K 10 2
◇ 4 3
♣ A K 10 9

♠ K 7 5   ♠ 10 4 2
♡ 6 5 4   ♡ J 3
◇ 10 9 8 7 6   ◇ A K 5 2
♣ Q J   ♣ 8 7 6 5

♠ A Q J 3
♡ Q 9 8 7
◇ Q J
♣ 4 3 2

'Naturally,' concluded the Hideous Hog, 'this defence would have been wasted on the Walrus and his like. Even that Secretary Bird would only lose the contract when he is at the top of his form. But Papa is just right. He is, after all, a good player.'

'Well, it was a fine, imaginative defence,' said Oscar, 'and you would have fallen for it yourself, H.H., so you've no cause to jeer at Papa.'

The Hog shook his massive head vigorously.

'Don't you believe it, Oscar,' he replied in an injured voice, 'I would have ruffed in my hand, not in dummy. After the ace of trumps I would have played a small one to my hand. Had East shown out, I could have finessed against J x x x and I should have discarded my losing club—if I had a losing club—on dummy's long trump. Papa would have doubtless played the same way had he thought about it. The urge to be clever, to unravel my plot, proved too much for him. Some people can only think of their own thirteen cards. Others, like Papa, can only think of the twenty-six held by their opponents. All of us, that is, *nearly* all, have our faults.'

16. Seventh from the Left

'Do you think there may be something in it, after all?' asked the Rueful Rabbit as we drove home from the Griffins. 'I mean, this numerology business. Whatever the sceptics say, it does seem to work, doesn't it?' Dropping his voice, he added confidentially: 'Seven, you know, was my lucky number today, especially after nightfall. You'll find it under my sign, Virgo, in *The Stars Speak*, in tonight's paper.'

I could not help feeling that the Rabbit's interest in the occult had been stimulated by the last rubber of the evening. As seemed to happen so often, fate brought him together with the Hideous Hog. Arrayed against them were the Hog's favourite opponents, Papa the Greek and the Emeritus Professor of Bio-Sophistry, known to us all on account of his appearance as the Secretary Bird.

This was the first deal:

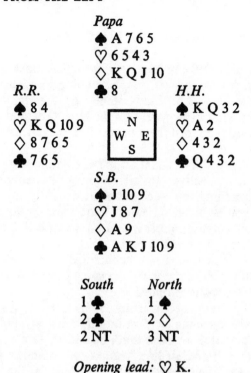

Papa
♠ A 7 6 5
♡ 6 5 4 3
◇ K Q J 10
♣ 8

R.R.
♠ 8 4
♡ K Q 10 9
◇ 8 7 6 5
♣ 7 6 5

H.H.
♠ K Q 3 2
♡ A 2
◇ 4 3 2
♣ Q 4 3 2

S.B.
♠ J 10 9
♡ J 8 7
◇ A 9
♣ A K J 10 9

South	North
1 ♣	1 ♠
2 ♣	2 ◇
2 NT	3 NT

Opening lead: ♡ K.

The Hog overtook the ♡ K and returned the ♡ 2. After
gathering four tricks with effortless ease, the Rabbit paused to
regroup. He had an uncanny feeling that his partner had not
followed to the last heart. It could even be that he had shown out
before. But if so, what had he discarded? The Rueful Rabbit
could not be sure and he did not like to ask. It was undignified
and he knew from experience that the information was rarely
worth the supercilious smiles which went with it.

'By all means, look at the last trick. Look at the lot—if it will
convey anything to you,' somebody would say, and there would be
sniggers all round.

After a close study of dummy, the Rabbit was inclined to lead a
spade. But what if S.B. wrapped up four spade tricks quickly and
followed up with five more—on a finesse perhaps—in clubs? And
then it might transpire that all the time H.H. had the ◇ A! How

was one to tell? R,R's mind wandered from suit to suit before drifting gently to astrology, the Stock Exchange and kindred topics.

'He's thinking!' broke in the Hideous Hog in mock alarm. 'We are truly lost, for as you can see, he's going to do his best. No hope now that he will hit inadvertently on the right card. Oh, please stop thinking, R.R.,' went on the Hog, 'just shut your eyes, open your mouth and lead the seventh from the left. It's safer that way.'

The Rabbit gulped. His adam's apple oscillating angrily, his lips compressed, his sensitive nostrils aquiver, he counted up to seven, and detaching the ♣ 6, waved it defiantly in the air. 'It would serve you right,' he cried, 'if I took you at your word. It would sink our defence, but it would be worth it if it taught you not to be rude till the hand is over.'

There was a dangerous gleam behind S.B's pince-nez. The wild tufts of hair to which he owed his nickname projected belligerently from his low dome-shaped head.

'The ♣ 6,' he announced in hostile, sibilant tones, 'is an exposed card within the meaning of Section 39. Law 50 applies. I call upon you to play it, R.R. And that', he added, with a malevolent curve of his thin, bloodless lips, 'should be a lesson to you both.'

No one spoke. The Greek glared suspiciously at the Hog. Why was he so strangely quiet? Why wasn't he insulting someone? It was not natural and Papa did not like it.

With shaking fingers and a scornful look at the Professor, the Rabbit flung the ♣ 6 on the table. 'Give unto Caesar . . .' murmured the Hog softly, following with the ♣ 2.

The Professor made eight tricks—three clubs, four diamonds and the ♠ A. One down.

'Unmakeable,' he observed.

'Unloseable,' rejoined H.H.

'Ssss,' hissed the Secretary Bird venomously. Oscar cleared his throat and was about to say something.

'Exactly,' agreed the Hog, 'if only the Emeritus Professor had not been so insistent on that ♣ 6, the ninth trick would have fallen automatically into his lap. Whether R.R. had continued with a spade or a diamond, the five-card end-position would have been the same. Let us say, that left to his own devices, he would have led a spade. What happens? The ace is taken. Three diamonds are cashed and here you are:

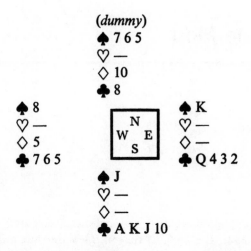

(*dummy*)
♠ 7 6 5
♡ —
◇ 10
♣ 8

♠ 8
♡ —
◇ 5
♣ 7 6 5

N
W   E
S

♠ K
♡ —
◇ —
♣ Q 4 3 2

♠ J
♡ —
◇ —
♣ A K J 10

Dummy's last diamond squeezes me in the black suits and the club finesse brings home the contract. Fortunately,' he added with a friendly leer, 'you—er—he broke up the impending squeeze with that well-timed ♣ 6. Was it really the seventh from the left? Ha! ha!'

17. Vive le Mort

'The dice are loaded against the defence,' declared the Hog, shaking his head. 'It stands to reason. Declarer has a dummy, *le mort* as the French say, while a defender must always look over his shoulder at a live partner. What chance has he?'

We were sitting at the bar of the Unicorn, waiting for M. Merle to take our orders for dinner. The Hog was in a chastened mood, induced no doubt by thoughts of the rigorous diet which he was about to put into operation—no soft drinks, virtually no refreshments between lunch and tea, and no foie gras at all, except on week days.

'*Le mort*,' he resumed wistfully, 'if only a defender could have one, too, what a difference it would make to the average player! Even for the master it would transform the game. Mind you,' went on the Hideous Hog, modestly casting down his thick ginger eyelashes, 'with a great artist at the helm, success does not demand that partner should be an absolute corpse. A zombie will do. So long as he does not try to think for himself, his side is bound to have a chance.'

As he came to the end of his soliloquy, the Hog wrote down a hand.

'Well, now, Oscar,' he said, passing a diagram with the North and East hands to the Owl, 'what are your prospects of defeating 4 ♠?'

♠ J 10
♡ 6 5 4 3
◇ A Q J
♣ A Q J 9

```
            ┌─────────┐   ♠ 3 2
            │    N    │   ♡ A 8 7
            │ W     E │   ◇ 5 4 3 2
            │    S    │   ♣ K 10 8 7
            └─────────┘
```

West	North	East	South
			Pass
Pass	1 ♣	Pass	1 ♠
Pass	1 NT	Pass	4 ♠

Opening lead: ♡ Q.

It seemed highly unlikely that West had opened a doubleton queen. Conceding the point, Oscar agreed to play the ♡ A. Declarer's card was the ten. Then came a prolonged pause. Fifty-six calories later—allowing for olives—there was still no progress and the Hideous Hog was back in the fray.

'Come, come, Oscar,' he said impatiently, 'you have made one trick, ♡ A and you expect to win another with the ♣ K. Partner has, of course, a trump trick.' H.H. paused, hoping that someone would ask him to explain. We sat tight, knowing that he needed no encouragement.

'Ah! well,' resumed the Hog, 'since you can't see it, I suppose I'd better dot the 'i's and cross the 't's. Where were we? Oh yes, of course. The lead of the ♡ Q pinpoints the ♡ K. Delcarer must have it since no one else has. Even you can see that. Next come the trumps. Declarer must have six of them, if not seven, for he jumped to 4 ♠ over 1 NT. Yet he passed as dealer. Why? Obviously he was missing the ♠ A or ♠ K. With A K Q to six and an out-side king he would have opened. He did not. Therefore he has not. It's as simple as that. And now, having identified your three certain defensive tricks—the ♡ A, the ♣ K and the king (or ace) of trumps—how do you set about getting a fourth?'

No one spoke.

'Have you considered a ruff?' suggested the Hog.

Oscar's round amber eyes widened in surprise. Peregrine the Penguin flapped a flipper impatiently. 'Ruff what?' he asked irritably.

'If you can't think of the best return,' pursued H.H., leering happily to left and right, 'think of the worst. Perhaps it will come more easily to you.'

'The worst would be a club,' ventured the Owl.

'To be precise, the ♣ 10,' agreed the Penguin.

'Am I to take it,' inquired H.H., drawing them on, 'that you would not lead the ♣ 10 in any circumstances?'

'Of course not,' said Oscar unanimously.

'But what if it were a singleton?' went on the Hog.

That, we agreed, would make all the difference. Since it was not a singleton, however, what was the good of pretending?

I forget who put the question, but the Hog turned on him at once. 'All the good in the world,' he answered vehemently. 'Think of it as a singleton. Tell your zombie opposite that it's a singleton and declarer will end up by thinking so, too. Why, he will say to himself, were it not a singleton no one would be so crazy as to lead it.'

Quickly filling in the other hands, the Hog invited us to look at the picture from declarer's point of view.

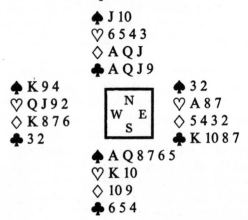

♠ J 10
♡ 6 5 4 3
◇ A Q J
♣ A Q J 9

♠ K 9 4   ♠ 3 2
♡ Q J 9 2   ♡ A 8 7
◇ K 8 7 6   ◇ 5 4 3 2
♣ 3 2   ♣ K 10 8 7

♠ A Q 8 7 6 5
♡ K 10
◇ 10 9
♣ 6 5 4

'Imagine that you are South. You've lost the first trick to the ♡ A and you've captured East's ♣ 10 with dummy's ♣ J. You lose the trump finesse to West's king and a club comes back. Do you go up with the ace? Of course not. You expect East to ruff, though it won't disturb you unduly, for you can afford it. After drawing trumps, you will finesse again and the fourth club will absorb your potential diamond loser.

'Of course, it won't work out that way. Instead of ruffing, East will win the club return with his king—the king he cannot possibly have—and continue with a third club which West will trump.'

The Owl was about to open his mouth, but the Hideous Hog was too quick for him. 'I wish you wouldn't always interrupt, Oscar. I know what you are thinking or rather what you should be thinking. You are wondering how I knew—for I was East, needless to say—that declarer would turn up with three clubs. Well, I didn't. But the bidding suggested that he had six spades and his ♡ 10 to the first trick indicated a doubleton. So I expected to find him with five cards in the minors and I was giving myself by far the best chance available. Mind you, it might not have worked with a live partner. Knowing that I could not have a singleton club—since that would leave declarer with six—he would have been sorely tempted to think up something clever on his own. Papa, no doubt, would have tried a diamond, away from his king. Luckily, I was playing with the Rabbit, who does not think and is too frightened not to return my suit.'

The Hog was looking almost pleased with life when the appearance of M. Merle brought him back with a jerk to grim reality.

'For me, something light and simple,' he said sadly to the maître d'hôtel, 'a sole Walevska, a pheasant Souvoroff and a chocolate mousse. I daren't cut it down further still,' he added apologetically, 'for it will have to last me all the way to supper.'

A Traumatic Defence

While we conferred with M. Merle about the immediate future, the Hog, pretending not to listen, was writing down another hand.

```
      ♠ 5 4 3 2        ┌─────────┐
      ♡ Q 10 9         │    N    │
      ◇ 7 6            │ W     E │
      ♣ K 10 9 6       │    S    │
                       └─────────┘
                  ♠ Q 6
                  ♡ 8 5 4 3
                  ◇ A J 2
                  ♣ 5 4 3 2
```

West	North	East	South
	1 ◇	2 ♠	Pass
3 ♠	Pass	4 ♠	

We were about to agree on a salmon trout *persane* when the Hog broke in to tell us the bidding.

'You are South,' he informed us. 'You lead the ◇ A and note partner's ten. How do you proceed to break the contract?'

'The best chance . . .' began Oscar, but H.H. would have none of it. 'No best chance about it,' he snapped. 'Give yourself the *only* chance.'

Oscar tried again. 'Partner could have a singleton heart. He comes in with the ♠ A, which he must then have for his opening bid, and puts me in with the ◇ J to give him a ruff. How about that?'

The Hog snorted. 'Just one trifling snag,' he observed, curving his lips downward in derision. 'If partner had a singleton heart, which he hasn't, and if it occurred to him to under-lead his ◇ K Q, which it would not, he could not ruff anything, anyway, for though, as you say, he would be marked on the bidding with the ace of trumps, he could hardly have another. You really can't expect declarer, you know, to have made a jump overcall on a five-card suit headed by the K J. And if he has six spades, partner's ace is bare. So let's try something sensible shall we?'

No one said a word. The Hog was feeling on top and enjoying himself accordingly. It warmed the cockles of his heart to know that all around him were his inferiors. Suddenly, from behind a pillar which concealed his diaphanous frame from view, came the voice of the Emeritus Professor of Bio-Sophistry.

'Very well,' he was saying to M. Merle, 'I'll have the *homard a l'armoricaine*, but nothing will persuade me that all this cream is fattening. I've lived on it for weeks and I haven't managed to put on an ounce.'

With a vicious snarl the Hideous Hog turned his back on the offending pillar.

'I was South,' he said, as if we had not guessed already. 'At trick two I led the *two* of diamonds to partner's queen. Of course, he was taken in completely. Thinking that I had no more diamonds, he led another, expecting me to ruff in the full knowledge that dummy's trumps were too low to ruff over me. My ♢ J came as a shock to him and it shocked him more still to see declarer enjoy a ruff and discard. But my traumatic defence was crowned with glory almost at once for partner was still under the spell when he came in with the ace of trumps and he promptly played another diamond. Sitting with the queen, now bare, over declarer's king of trumps, I got my ruff. This was the deal:

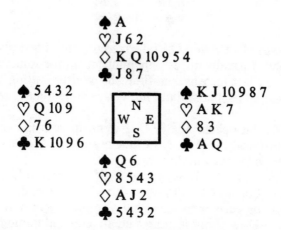

```
                  ♠ A
                  ♡ J 6 2
                  ♢ K Q 10 9 5 4
                  ♣ J 8 7
   ♠ 5 4 3 2          N          ♠ K J 10 9 8 7
   ♡ Q 10 9       W       E      ♡ A K 7
   ♢ 7 6              S          ♢ 8 3
   ♣ K 10 9 6                    ♣ A Q
                  ♠ Q 6
                  ♡ 8 5 4 3
                  ♢ A J 2
                  ♣ 5 4 3 2
```

'Observe the difference between this hand and the last,' went on the Hog, barely pausing to devour a handful of olives. 'On the previous deal my object was to deceive declarer, and partner did not matter at all. This time I had to fool partner and declarer didn't come into it. Yet both times the same principle applied. Pulling the strings from across the table I played partner's cards—the only way to play them, of course.'

I

Entries Out of Thin Air

Drawing on the morrow for an advance of 50 calories, the Hog accepted another glass of Madeira and put down this hand.

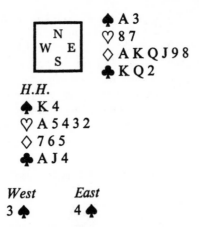

♠ A 3
♡ 8 7
◇ A K Q J 9 8
♣ K Q 2

H.H.
♠ K 4
♡ A 5 4 3 2
◇ 7 6 5
♣ A J 4

West	East
3 ♠	4 ♠

'I need hardly tell you,' he informed us, 'that I was playing with the Rabbit. I usually do. It's my punishment for something awful I did in my last incarnation. Still, the Walrus, sitting West, was against me, so I suppose that I must have done some decent things, too.

'The Rabbit opened the ♡ Q. I went up with the ace and the Walrus dropped the king. Now take my seat and tell me how you set about collecting another three tricks.'

Nothing immediately suggested itself and before long the Hog was prompting us. 'I will give you a clue,' he said, 'there's not much left for partner to have, but you must give him credit for something. How about leading a small club and finding him with the ten? That will force out one of dummy's honours. When partner leads the suit again, through the other, we shall make two tricks with the ace and knave before declarer can go gay with all those luscious diamonds.'

'But how can partner ever get in to lead through dummy?' objected the Penguin, 'he has no possible entry?'

'You can conjure up entries out of thin air,' declared H.H., waving Oscar's cigar like a wand. 'At least, I can.'

A word was beginning to form on the Penguin's lips.

'Since you can't see it, I'll tell you. I put partner in with a trump,' vouchsafed the Hog. 'That's where the thin air came in. There was little more for partner to have, but there was just room for the ♠ Q. It was the only hope, so I concentrated on hoping. On dummy's ace of trumps I threw my king and my hopes were rewarded when partner captured the next trick with the queen and pierced dummy's gizzard with a club.'

This was the complete deal:

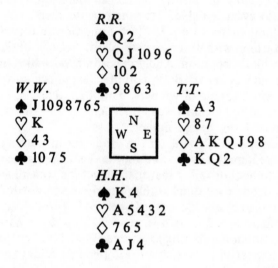

```
                    R.R.
                    ♠ Q 2
                    ♡ Q J 10 9 6
                    ◇ 10 2
   W.W.             ♣ 9 8 6 3      T.T.
   ♠ J 10 9 8 7 6 5                ♠ A 3
   ♡ K              ┌──────┐       ♡ 8 7
   ◇ 4 3            │  N   │       ◇ A K Q J 9 8
   ♣ 10 7 5         │W   E │       ♣ K Q 2
                    │  S   │
                    └──────┘
                    H.H.
                    ♠ K 4
                    ♡ A 5 4 3 2
                    ◇ 7 6 5
                    ♣ A J 4
```

'But the Rabbit didn't have the ♣ 10,' protested Oscar, 'and surely everything hinged on it?'

'True,' agreed the Hog, 'but that was no reflection on my plan. The Rabbit had to make do with the ♣ 9, but it proved just as effective since the Walrus did not think of going up with his ten, as he should have done.

'Such is life,' added H.H., philosophically. 'One does not expect anything from partner. But one is entitled to a little assistance from declarer. After all, everyone can't always be on the other side.'

18. A Spirited Defence

'Double dummy problems!' exclaimed the Hog, breathing contempt into every syllable. 'Anyone can do them, that is if they have nothing better to do. It's just a question of time. Try everything, starting with the weirdest plays. Sooner or later you're bound to hit the solution. And you needn't waste time on anything that anyone would ever do in real life. Just chuck away an ace or two. Trump a couple of winners. You'll get there in the end.'

The bar at the Griffins was almost empty and this was our last magnum of Krug before dinner.

'Those problems,' went on the Hog, 'mean nothing at all for they ignore human reflexes and they make no allowance for speed. Neither do textbooks for that matter, yet it's sometimes better to play the wrong card quickly than the right one slowly.'

Encouraged by our silence the Hideous Hog proceeded to explain.

'Sometimes speed is its own reward. You don't have to know what you are doing so long as you do it quickly. Try this hand on which I happened to be sitting East a couple of days ago.'

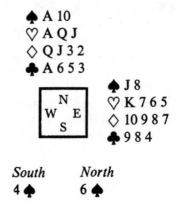

```
          ♠ A 10
          ♡ A Q J
          ◇ Q J 3 2
          ♣ A 6 5 3
                         ♠ J 8
          ┌─────┐        ♡ K 7 6 5
          │  N  │        ◇ 10 9 8 7
          │W   E│        ♣ 9 8 4
          │  S  │
          └─────┘

        South      North
        4 ♠        6 ♠
```

'West opens the ♣ Q which declarer wins with the king in the closed hand. He leads the ♡ 10 and plays dummy's queen. What should you do?'

'Return a diamond,' volunteered the Toucan. 'Declarer may be hoping to get rid of a losing diamond on a heart.'

'I duck' hazarded Oscar the Owl. 'It's usually the correct technique.'

'I, too, duck,' declared the Rabbit with unaccustomed confidence.

'Why?' asked H.H.

'Because', explained R.R., 'no one in a slam would really think of ducking, so unless I was intended to do something different, if you see what I mean, you wouldn't be asking me, would you?'

'True,' conceded the Hog, snorting gracefully. 'Yet neither you nor Oscar have a clue as to what it's all about. You haven't asked yourselves, any of you, why declarer should embark on the heart finesse, before drawing trumps. Yet that is surely the key to it all, "the dog that didn't bark in the night" as Edgar Allan Poe put it— or was it Simenon? Anyway, if declarer wanted to get rid of a diamond, he could do it *after* drawing trumps. That's why Timothy gave the wrong answer. You and Oscar gave the right one, though for the wrong reason or rather for no reason at all. And yet you would have beaten the contract, just as I did. The mere fact that you didn't know what you were doing would have made no difference, so long as you did it quickly. This was the deal:

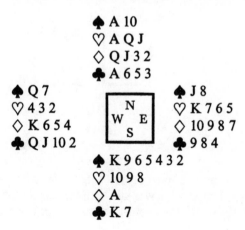

```
                    ♠ A 10
                    ♡ A Q J
                    ◇ Q J 3 2
                    ♣ A 6 5 3
        ♠ Q 7                      ♠ J 8
        ♡ 4 3 2         N          ♡ K 7 6 5
        ◇ K 6 5 4   W     E        ◇ 1 0 9 8 7
        ♣ Q J 10 2      S          ♣ 9 8 4
                    ♠ K 9 6 5 4 3 2
                    ♡ 1 0 9 8
                    ◇ A
                    ♣ K 7
```

'Now you can see why declarer took the heart finesse before touching trumps,' said the Hog, certain that no one could see anything. 'If the finesse succeeded, he could afford a safety play in trumps. If it failed, he couldn't. It was as simple as that.'

'What happened?' asked the Toucan eagerly.

'Naturally,' replied the Hog, who was hoping that someone would have the decency to ask him, 'declarer crossed back to his hand with a diamond ruff and led a trump, inserting dummy's ten to ensure himself against a 4–0 trump break. He did, too, of course, in a manner of speaking. But he couldn't ensure himself against my having the ♡ K, which came into its own in due course— after I had made my knave of trumps.'

'I need not point out,' pointed out the Hog, 'how fatal it would have been for me to pause, even for a few seconds, before playing low to the first round of hearts. It would have given the whole show away and declarer would never have considered that safety play which meant so much to my knave.'

Find the Lady

Emptying someone's glass absent-mindedly, the Hog wrote down another hand and passed it round.

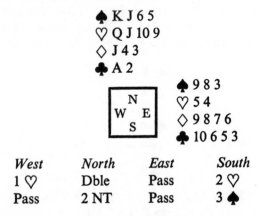

```
                  ♠ K J 6 5
                  ♡ Q J 10 9
                  ◇ J 4 3
                  ♣ A 2
                              ♠ 9 8 3
                   N          ♡ 5 4
                W     E       ◇ 9 8 7 6
                   S          ♣ 10 6 5 3
```

West	North	East	South
1 ♡	Dble	Pass	2 ♡
Pass	2 NT	Pass	3 ♠

'North-South had a part-score, which is why the bidding stopped at 3 ♠, I suppose. I was sitting East, as you have probably guessed since those are the sort of hands I hold most of the time.

Anyway, partner started with the ♥ K and ♥ A, the ◊ K and
◊ A, on which declarer threw the queen, and a third diamond to
dummy's knave. Everyone followed to everything and our side
had taken four tricks. At this point declarer led dummy's ♥ Q.
Over to you.' With a sweeping gesture, H.H. took us all in.

'I ruff and return the ♣ 10,' suggested Timothy the Toucan.

The Hog greeted the suggestion strictly on its merits. With a
half-hearted sneer, he turned away.

'Trump with the nine to promote something,' ventured the Rabbit.

'I discard a club,' announced O.O., some ten seconds later.

'Perhaps . . .' I began.

'You are all hopelessly wrong,' declared H.H.

'Impossible,' protested the Owl. 'Between us we have covered
every solution and none at all. One of us must be right.'

'Not at all,' retorted the Hog, 'for you all took ages, over twenty
seconds, in fact, and that's inexcusable. But first let me ask you,
Oscar, why didn't you trump that ♥ Q?

'Because,' explained the Owl, 'I suspect that this hand is a little
like the last one. If declarer wants to discard a loser he can do so
after drawing trumps. More likely, he is concerned about the
trumps. Maybe he is missing the queen and hopes that I will give
myself away by ruffing if my trump holding is worthless and
refusing to ruff if I have the queen. To protect partner who has, presumably, that missing queen, I refuse to ruff. Q.E.D. Quite simple.'

'Too simple,' broke in the Hog. 'So simple, in fact, that had you
really started with Q x x you wouldn't have taken so long to
decide what to do. That pause of yours showed clearly that you
didn't have the queen.'

'How clever!' cried T.T., admiringly. 'You could see it all at a
glance and you played quickly, as you always do, and you didn't
ruff as R.R., and I would have done and. . . .'

'Oh, but I did ruff,' interrupted the Hog baring his teeth in what
may have been intended as a smile.

'But surely. . . .'

'I mean to say. . . .'

T.T. and R.R. protested simultaneously.

'Only, you see,' went on H.H. softly, 'my holding wasn't 9 8 3,
but Q 9 3, and I ruffed precisely because it seemed so foolish a
thing to do. But I did it in a jiffy and declarer didn't think that

anyone would be so clever so quickly. It was all a question of
speed, as I've been telling you. The same play in the same situation
may convey several different messages. It's just a matter of timing.'

Emilio, our barman, came round to remove the empty magnum.

'No,' said H.H., shaking his head hesitantly, 'I don't think that
I should have any more.'

'. . . er . .' . murmured the Toucan—or perhaps he was only
clearing his throat.

'Well, if you absolutely insist,' said the Hog, 'I'll make an
exception as it's so near Christmas.

Watching the Watch

'Mind you,' resumed the Hog, mellowing at the sight of another
bottle, 'you can be too quick as well as too slow, and you can be
one and t'other on the same hand, but the worst thing, of course,
is to play quickly when you should play slowly and vice versa.'
As he spoke, the Hog sketched another diagram with the North-
South hands. 'There you are.' he said. 'The bidding is straightforward—1 NT from South, 3 NT from North. West leads the
♠ 6.' The Hideous Hog placed his watch ostentatiously on the
table and prodded R.R. in the ribs.

♠ A 4
♡ A 10 2
◇ A 9 8 4 3 2
♣ 5 4

```
      N
   W     E
      S
```

♠ K J 3 2
♡ K 6 5 4
◇ K 7
♣ K 3 2

South	North
1 NT	3 NT

The Rabbit took a quick look. 'You can put that watch away,' he told H.H. 'I don't propose to detain you long. No doubt there's something devilish afoot, especially in diamonds. Just the same, I'll have the ♠ 4 from dummy and whatever card East plays. . . .'

'The eight,' said the Hog.

'. . . I win and lead the ◇ K.'

'The ◇ Q from West,' called H.H.

'I continue with the ◇ 7.'

'West plays the ten.'

'I duck,' said the Rabbit firmly.

'East overtakes with the knave and leads the ♣ Q. Curtains,' declared the Hog.

'I spoke too quickly,' admitted R.R. 'I go up with the ◇ A and play another.'

The Hideous Hog smiled happily. 'You are sunk, my friend, whatever you do. East wins the third diamond and shoots the ♣ Q as before.'

The Rabbit frowned. 'You mean there's nothing devilish about the diamonds?' he asked suspiciously.

'Nothing whatever,' the Hog assured him. 'You went down against perfectly innocuous breaks all round—but only because *I* was defending, so don't distress yourself. You took no more than twenty-five seconds over the first two tricks, which means that most of the time you would have made the contract. To think of unblocking with the ◇ Q most Wests would need twenty seconds at least and that king of yours flashed across the table in half that time. West would follow with the ten and you would let him hold the next trick with the queen, and that would be that. And it's no good saying that a defender can take his time, no matter how fast declarer plays. Apart from the psychological disadvantage of being outpaced, there is always the fear that a pause will give something away. No, no, speed was of the essence. Wasn't it Desdemona or Juliet or someone, who once said: "If it were done when 'tis done, then 'twere well it were done quickly?" For all that,' went on H.H., 'had you stopped to think longer when dummy went down, you wouldn't have been so pressed for time later.'

The Rabbit, whose mind hadn't wandered for nearly a minute,

had an idea. 'Perhaps,' he suggested brightly, 'I should have
ducked in both hands to that first spade.'

'Ingenious. Quite natty,' conceded the Hideous Hog, 'it might
even have worked for no one would know what was happening.
But there's a better way. Resisting the routine temptation to
ensure a third spade trick by letting the lead run up to your hand,
go up with dummy's ace at once. Then lead the deuce of diamonds,
finessing the seven unless East goes up with an honour.' The Hog
filled in the four hands.

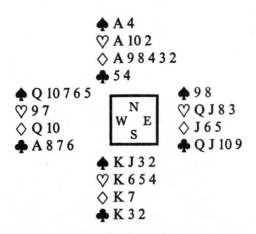

'Observe,' continued the Hog, 'that even if East starts with
◊ J 10 5 and is smart enough to go up with an honour, you're
still home unless West has the wits to throw his queen under your
king. To beat you both defenders must play well, in fact, very well,
and is that likely?'

19. The Hog Picks Papa

'Bridge players are no better than the rest of society,' said the Hideous Hog, gazing gloomily at the empty bottle. 'We're falling into grooves, repeating ourselves all the time. No imagination. Take this delusion that you obtain your best results when you play with your favourite partner. . . .'

'And so you do,' interjected Peregrine the Penguin defiantly. Fortified by Bollinger and Beluga, P.P. was prepared to stand up to anyone.

'What you mean', countered the Hog, 'is that opponents obtain their worst results against seasoned pairs. But to accept their gifts isn't the same thing as to conjure up tricks from nowhere by sheer artistry,'

'But if you can't get your best results with your favourite partner, when do you get them?' asked Oscar the Owl, our Senior Kibitzer.

'When you come up against your favourite opponents, of course,' retorted H.H., 'but being a lot of sheep we haven't devised a single competition in which you can choose your opponents. Be it pairs or teams or what have you, the emphasis is always on the over-rated partner figure. An arid, negative approach to the game,' continued the Hog. 'Why, let me pick my opponents and you can saddle me with any partner you like.'

The Hog's eyes rested on R.R. 'Excuse me,' he said, deftly extracting a large envelope which was protruding from the Rabbit's pocket. 'I want to show you a hand.' A few seconds later we were looking at these North-South cards.

North
♠ Q J 6
♡ 10 7 4
◇ 6 5 3
♣ Q 8 6 5

```
      N
   W     E
      S
```

♠ A 10 9 8 7
♡ A K Q J 5
◇ 7 4
♣ K

South	West	North	East
2 ♠	3 ♣	Pass	Pass
3 ♡	Pass	3 ♠	Pass
4 ♠			

'I happened to be South,' said the Hog. 'West led out the three
top diamonds, East petering to show four, and I ruffed the third
one. Your move, my friends.'

'Sooner or later we shall have to take that trump finesse,' said
the Penguin.

'Meanwhile,' suggested the Owl, 'let's try the ♣ K. One never
knows.'

'Quite right,' agreed the Hog. 'West may duck, thinking that I
am trying to create an entry in dummy. After all, he doesn't know
that I can always get there with the ♡ 10.' When his glass had
been refilled, H.H. continued. 'West, however, goes up smartly
with the ♣ A, East following with the two, and returns another
club, the knave to be precise. What next?'

'The trump finesse,' persisted the Penguin, 'you can't avoid it,
so get it over quickly.'

Oscar the Owl blinked non-committally.

The Rueful Rabbit looked suspicious. Only players like himself
took simple finesses, so that must be wrong.

'Peregrine is quite right,' declared H.H. 'Playing with your favourite dummy there is no alternative. You must finesse.'

The Penguin looked superior. 'Fortunately,' went on H.H. 'I was playing against my favourite opponent, the one I would pick. . . .'

'Papa,' said all in unison.

'Exactly,' the Hog smiled at the recollection, 'and now, you see, instead of taking an ordinary, prosaic finesse and going down, you go up with the ♠ A, drop West's bare king and . . .'

'Why should you?' demanded the Penguin.

'Because,' replied H.H., 'Papa has gone to a lot of trouble to provide you with an entry in dummy. He doesn't know that you can get there, anyway, or course, but he does know that your ♣ K was bare. . . .'

'Yes,' broke in the Rabbit, 'it's a funny thing how often the ♣ K is a singleton. Why only yesterday. . . .'

The Hog silenced him with a withering look and went on: 'His partner's deuce showed three clubs and he must have had five himself since he bid the suit at the Three level. No, there was no mystery about the clubs, but Papa must have wondered why I didn't draw trumps. The only reason could be that I wanted to play them from dummy, so he would do his best to keep me out of it—unless he had the king himself and wanted me to take the finesse.'

O.O. hooted softly.

'You see', went on H.H., 'what a difference it makes when you can have the opponent of your choice. Had the Toucan or the Walrus or even that Secretary Bird played the ♣ J, it wouldn't have been safe to deduce anything, for they wouldn't know what I had or what made me play as I did. But Papa was good enough to know everything—except that the ♡ 10 was an entry—and he was clever enough to give me a chance to go wrong. The reason I like playing against him so much,' concluded the Hog, 'is because he is so predictable. He does exactly what I would do myself, though nothing like so well, of course.'

This was the deal in full:

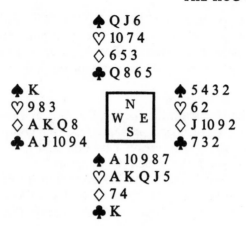

♠ Q J 6
♡ 10 7 4
◇ 6 5 3
♣ Q 8 6 5

♠ K   ♠ 5 4 3 2
♡ 9 8 3   ♡ 6 2
◇ A K Q 8   ◇ J 10 9 2
♣ A J 10 9 4   ♣ 7 3 2

♠ A 10 9 8 7
♡ A K Q J 5
◇ 7 4
♣ K

A Creative Contract

The Hog started writing down another hand, crossed something
out, began again, but evidently went wrong a second time. 'Give
me a bit of paper, someone,' he said irritably, crumpling up the
Rabbit's envelope and throwing it away in disgust.

'Please, H.H., could I have my share certificates back,' asked the
Rabbit ruefully. 'I know they've gone down already, but I've only
just received them and my broker says. . . .'

Nobody was listening to him. The barman had provided H.H.
with a pad and we were looking at this hand:

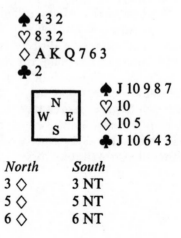

♠ 4 3 2
♡ 8 3 2
◇ A K Q 7 6 3
♣ 2

♠ J 10 9 8 7
♡ 10
◇ 10 5
♣ J 10 6 4 3

North	South
3 ◇	3 NT
5 ◇	5 NT
6 ◇	6 NT

'What extraordinary bidding!' exclaimed the Penguin in shocked tones.

The Owl blinked accusingly, his round amber eyes registering disapproval.

'There were—er—exceptional circumstances,' explained the Hog apologetically, 'but don't worry about the bidding. Concentrate on the defence West opened the ♡ 5 and I won with the ♡ Q. Yes, I was declarer. At trick two I played the ♠ 5, West playing the ♠ 6 and east was in with the ♠ 7. What card should he return?'

'Declarer's play can mean one thing only,' said the Penguin with aplomb, 'he is rectifying the count for a squeeze. Clearly, he wouldn't lead a low spade away from the three top honours, so his spade holding must be A 5 or more likely A K 5. If he has a doubleton diamond we can do nothing, for the suit breaks kindly, but if he has a singleton, he may be in trouble.'

'I agree,' said O.O., 'declarer's play indicates that he is short of a trick and is looking for a squeeze in the red suits, though it could be in clubs and diamonds.'

'So what do you do?' persisted the Hog. 'What would Papa do if he were East?'

'It's a classical situation,' answered the Penguin, jerking an authoritative flipper. 'East must return the ◇ 10 to break up the theoretical squeeze. That cuts declarer's communications with dummy, confines him to three diamond tricks and allows the defender who guards two suits to throw a diamond.'

'A likely hand for declarer,' suggested O.O., 'would be: ♠ A K 5 ♡ A K Q 4 ◇ 2 ♣ A K Q 7 5. If so, when West has to come down to four cards, he cannot retain the long heart as well as four diamonds.'

All agreed.

'Unfortunately,' sighed H.H., 'East wasn't Papa, but that Walrus, the points tycoon. Having 2 points only, he wasn't very interested in the defence, and anyway, he doesn't go in for breaking up squeezes. He returned another spade and. . . .'

'. . . and you made your cotranct, as usual, on a clever squeeze,' said the Rabbit admiringly.

'But where was Papa?' asked P.P., 'I thought this was another hand to illustrate your theory about favourite opponents.'

'And so it is,' declared the Hog. 'But Papa wasn't my opponent, except in the sense that he was my partner. That, of course, explains the unusual bidding sequence. Observe his low cunning. Why does he make a three bid, which we play as a weak, broken suit, knave high maybe, when he has the tops? Because he is afraid that I might bid no trumps and play the hand, and he thinks that I won't dare to do that without the tops in his suit. Since he has them himself, I can't have them, too, so I can't bid no trumps and I will be forced to let him play the hand, which is his prime objective in every deal. But as you can see he didn't fool me,' added the Hog, filling in the other two hands:

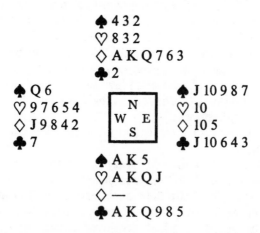

♠ 4 3 2
♡ 8 3 2
◇ A K Q 7 6 3
♣ 2

♠ Q 6
♡ 9 7 6 5 4
◇ J 9 8 4 2
♣ 7

N
W   E
S

♠ J 10 9 8 7
♡ 10
◇ 10 5
♣ J 10 6 4 3

♠ A K 5
♡ A K Q J
◇ —
♣ A K Q 9 8 5

'A void in partner's suit. That is going too far,' remonstrated the Owl.

'Preposterous,' snapped the Penguin.

'Unpardonable,' said the Hog. 'Having opened 3 ◇ he should have had the decency to pass my 3 NT. Still, that wasn't my fault and I couldn't very well help having a void, could I? But you see how important it is to have the right opponents at this game. Had Papa been East, I should have brought off a remarkable coup. Against that unimaginative Walrus, no artist can be creative.'

'Oh, I don't know,' said the Rabbit. 'Without Papa as your partner you would never have reached so creative a contract. I mean, it takes two wrongs to make a right, doesn't it?'

20. Starring the Villains

'The Blue Team wins through sheer, undiluted luck,' declared the Hideous Hog, twirling viciously the stem of his ever-empty glass. 'For don't forget that no match can be won before it is lost and the Italians just haven't a player capable of doing it.'

'You mean . . .' began Oscar the Owl, our Senior Kibitzer.

'Yes, I certainly do,' agreed H.H. with feeling. 'The speed of a convoy is determined by the speed of the slowest ship. No team can play better than its weakest member will allow and it follows that if there's no weakest member, there's precious little merit in winning. Your Italians simply happen to have fluked their way into stumbling on six non-losers. It's as if some team contrived somehow to pick six Me's!'

A shudder ran through the company.

'But observe the difference,' went on the Hog. 'I am expected to win even when I play with the Rabbit. The Garozzos and Forquets carry the day only when they are harnessed to Belladonnas, Pabis-Ticcis and their like. What I want to see,' concluded the Hog, thumping the table, 'is Bobby Wolff performing on Bridgerama, not with Bob Hamman, but with Timothy the Toucan or Robinson facing, not Jordan, but Walter the Walrus or. . . .'

'I have an idea,' broke in Peregrine the Penguin, Senior Kibitzer at the Unicorn. From the abrupt flipper-like movements of his short thick arms to the orange bow tie, surmounting the convex line of a snowy white shirt, everything about Peregrine dovetailed with his nick-name.

'How would it be', he went on, 'if to mark the tercentenary of the Unicorn, we had a match starring the losers. Just for once the spotlight would be on the villains rather than on the heroes. The Rabbit would choose one team and the Walrus would pick the

K

other, and whichever side recruited H.H. would have the Toucan as a counterweight.'

The Hideous Hog snorted appreciatively. To be rated as high as the Toucan was low, was no mean compliment and it only needed the lure of a case of Krug '64, offered by Oscar as a prize for the best individual performance, to overcome his moral scruples against playing not for money. 'I suppose', he said graciously, 'someone in my position must make sacrifices for the public good.'

I was late for the match and missed the first two boards. 'Who's leading?' I asked O.O.

'Don't know yet,' replied the Owl. 'There's been a bit of a mix-up and they're still trying to sort it out. Both East-West and North-South seem to have made game in hearts on the first board and both have made twelve tricks in no trumps on the second. Evidently something's wrong somewhere.'

'The Rabbit has misboarded,' I suggested. But that wasn't the explanation. This was the story which emerged when we were able to check on the facts.

```
                        T.T.
                        ♠ K Q 10 9 8 7 5
                        ♡ K J
                        ◇ 5 3 2
         W.W.           ♣ 2              S.B.
         ♠ 4 3                           ♠ A J
         ♡ —         ┌─────────┐         ♡ Q 9 7 5 3
         ◇ K J 10 7 6 4 │  N      │      ◇ Q 9 8
         ♣ A 10 9 6 5 │W   E│         ♣ K Q 8
                       │   S     │
                       └─────────┘
                        C.C.
                        ♠ 6 2
                        ♡ A 10 8 6 4 2
                        ◇ A
                        ♣ J 7 4 3
```

South	West	North	East
1 ♡	1 NT	Dble	2 ♡
Dble	ALL PASS		

The final contract was due to a series of misunderstandings. W.W's overcall was the Unusual No Trump. As he explained scornfully when it was all over, there was no reason why the Unusual No Trump should be Two No Trumps. He was a simple, sensible player who didn't use the plural when he intended the singular or vice versa. He wanted his partner to show his better and longer minor, and that's all there was to it.

Timothy the Toucan doubled to show that his side held the balance of strength. The situation presented no problem. Not so for the Emeritus Professor of Bio-Sophistry who crossed, then uncrossed his long, wiry legs and glared suspiciously at all and sundry from behind his pince-nez. Looking more than ever like a Secretary Bird, with wild tufts of hair projecting at right angles from his low-domed head, he hissed under his breath. Something sinister was afoot. There just couldn't be so many high cards in one pack—an opening bid, an overcall, a double and 14 excellent points left over for himself.

To bring matters into the open and to gain time, S.B. bid 2 ♡. The Walrus heaved his bulky frame from side to side, but before he could so much as break a coffee cup, Colin the Corgi doubled and that let Walter out. He had asked his partner to pick a minor and he had no intention of being landed with the baby himself. Fortunately, after the double, he could thrust the baby back where it belonged. His pass conveyed the pregnant message.

The Professor, alas, saw it in a different light. His partner's no trump proclaimed a stop, probably a double stop in hearts. Obviously the overcall was genuine for otherwise he would have taken appropriate action over the double. So when the Toucan passed, the Secretary Bird passed too. The Walrus gasped and the scorer dropped his pencil.

Colin the Corgi, who had watched the pantomime with detached amusement, knew precisely what had happened and to extract the maximum penalty he opened his ace of trumps. The Toucan's knave did nothing to put him off and he continued with a second trump to the king. T.T. now led his ♠ K, but it was too late. The Professor won with the ace and took four rounds of clubs, negotiating successfully the marked finesse and discarding his spade. A spade ruff in the closed hand brought his total of tricks to six and he still had the ♡ Q 9 under declarer's ♡ 10 8 6 4. At

trick nine, S.B. led a diamond to Colin's ace. With trumps only
left C.C. was obliged to play into the Professor's tenace.

'Sorry, partner,' apologized the Toucan. 'Of course I should
have taken it out, but I thought for a moment that your double
was for penalties!'

H.H. Protects His Image

In the other room the auction took a different course.

South	West	North	East
Papa	R.R.	Karapet	H.H.
1 ♡	2 ◇	2 ♠	2 NT
3 ♡	4 ◇	4 ♡	Dble

Like S.B., the Hideous Hog was thoroughly suspicious of the
bidding. There seemed to be too many aces and kings about. Not
trusting anyone, he bid a modest 2 NT to make sure that if the
worst came to the worst, he would at least give himself the best
chance of playing the hand.

Papa didn't like to bid 3 ♡, but he felt sure that the Hog was
spoofing, bidding no trumps on the strength of a diamond fit. If
he, Papa, didn't rebid hearts, no one would do it for him and the
wrong man might end up in charge of the contract.

Having played with Papa for years, Karapet, the Free Armenian, decided wisely that it was better to raise Papa's hearts to four
than to rebid his comparatively short seven-card suit. After all,
he didn't want to end up in 5 ♡.

To the Hog it looked as if he had three or four tricks to spare
for his double. Maybe it was unsporting to shoot at sitting birds,
but then no one had asked the birds to sit—not in 4 ♡, anyway.

A diamond was led to Papa's singleton ace and H.H., coming
in at trick two with the ace of spades, played back another diamond. The Greek ruffed and led his ♣ J towards dummy. The
Rabbit's long sensitive nose twitched suspiciously. Feeling sure
that Papa had the K Q behind the knave, he went up with his ♣ A
and led a third diamond, allowing the Greek to ruff a second time
in his hand. Now came a spade to dummy's queen, dropping the
knave, and a third spade, ruffed by H.H. and overruffed in the

closed hand. Crossing to dummy with a club ruff, Papa played another spade ready to throw a losing club if the Hog didn't ruff. H.H. ruffed, however, and Papa once again overruffed. He had scored four trump tricks in his hand, by ruffing two diamonds and overruffing two spades and he was left with the ♡ A 10 and two clubs. He trumped a club in dummy with the ♡ K and led a spade. With trumps only left, the Hog ruffed. For the third time the Greek overruffed, bringing home his contract by making all six trumps in his own hand, two club ruffs in dummy, one spade and the ◊ A.

'Why didn't you lead a trump?' bellowed the Hog shaking his fist at the Rabbit. 'We could have murdered the contract.'

After the match, when feelings had cooled down, I reproved the Hog. 'A bit unfair, you know, H.H., to crime the Rabbit for not leading a trump when he didn't have one.'

'Bah!' replied the Hideous Hog, 'he didn't even try. Besides it's a question of morale. It so happens that I could have broken the contract myself by leading a trump when I was in with the ♠ A. It would have been bad for the side if someone had spotted it and accused me of slipping. That Rabbit is expected to blunder. After all, that's why he's captain, but for the sake of the team I had to protect my image. One has obligations, you know.'

What Went Wrong?

The second deal looked simple enough in Room 1 where Colin the Corgi sailed smoothly and quickly into game after the straight-forward sequence of: 1 NT–3 NT.

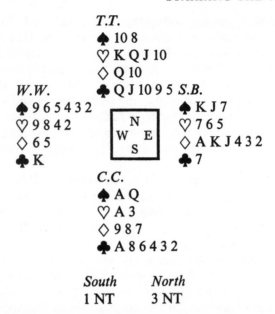

T.T.
♠ 10 8
♡ K Q J 10
◇ Q 10
♣ Q J 10 9 5

W.W.
♠ 9 6 5 4 3 2
♡ 9 8 4 2
◇ 6 5
♣ K

S.B.
♠ K J 7
♡ 7 6 5
◇ A K J 4 3 2
♣ 7

C.C.
♠ A Q
♡ A 3
◇ 9 8 7
♣ A 8 6 4 3 2

South	North
1 NT	3 NT

Walter the Walrus opened his fourth best spade to the king and ace, and Colin proceeded to wrap up twelve tricks—six clubs, four hearts and two spades.

'Nothing in it,' he observed, putting the cards back in their slots. 'A happy lead and every card that matters is right. Mind you,' he added, '5 ♣ is a better contract.'

In the other room the bidding was the same, but thereafter events took a very different course.

Still smarting from the Hog's rebuke for not opening a trump on the previous hand, the Rabbit felt deeply conscious of his responsibilities as captain. He knew that he was expected to set an example, not to sit back tamely doing the obvious, like not leading trumps. He knew, too, about the 11 rule or rather he knew that others knew about it, for he himself had little faith in higher mathematics. But he had heard recently that the all-conquering Italians followed some more sophisticated method—the fifth highest or the third lowest or something, and what was good enough for the *Squadra Azzurra* was good enough for him. Nodding to himself vigorously in Italian, the Rabbit led the ♠ 2.

As dummy came into view the Hog quickly weighed up the

hands. Papa's opening 1 NT showed 12–14 points. Dummy had 11 and he himself had 12. That left 3–5 for the Rabbit and it followed that if he had led from the ♠ A, he couldn't have either the king or the ace of clubs and in that case there was no hope whatever for the defence. The Hog was assuming, of course, that his partner's lead of the deuce indicated a four-card suit.

A successful defence had to be based on the supposition that declarer had the ♠ A, but would have to give up the lead in clubs before he could develop nine tricks. Even then it wouldn't all be plain-sailing. Trick one would go to Papa's ♠ A and trick two or three to the Rabbit's ace or king of clubs. But then, not knowing who had the ♠ J, R.R. would try to put his partner in to lead a spade through the closed hand, and in looking for an entry he was as likely to try one red suit as the other. In fact, a heart might look the safer of the two, and then declarer would spread his hand claiming the rest of the tricks. Could the danger be averted? A moment's thought and H.H. had the answer. Instead of going up with the ♠ K, he carefully played the ♠ J. He reasoned that seeing the ace take the knave, the Rabbit would do one of two things. He would either lead another spade, thinking it a safe thing to do or he would have the sense to switch to diamonds. And whichever he played, a diamond or a spade, the contract would be broken.

Of course, if Papa had the ♠ Q, as well as the ace, the far-sighted play of the knave would be even more effective. Placing the Greek with the three top honours the Rabbit would see at once that there was no future in spades and from that moment even he couldn't go wrong.

Papa, too, however, was thinking ahead. It was clear to him that, with the diamonds wide open, everything would hinge on the club position. Should he finesse or play for the drop? The odds were roughly even and for a player of Papa's quality that wasn't nearly good enough. Fortunately, the situation lent itself to a classical piece of deception. In the textbook example South takes East's knave not with the queen, but with the ace. West thinks, of course, that his partner has the queen and when he gains the lead he plays a small one away from his king.

Relying on this pretty stratagem, the Greek felt that the finesse was all but foolproof since even if it failed, the Rabbit would lead another spade, away from his king, instead of the dreaded diamond.

And so it came to pass. Winning the knave with the ace, Papa crossed to dummy with a heart and ran the ♣ Q to the Rabbit's king. Taken in as intended, R.R. returned a low spade. It looked to him as if the Hog had started with the ♠ Q J or maybe even with the K Q J, and anyway, a spade could do no harm. Amid gasps of astonishment from the kibitzers the Hog's king brought down Papa's lone queen. The burst of silence was broken by a loud guffaw from the Hideous Hog.

'Even you, my dear Themistocles, have never outwitted yourself to better purpose,' he jeered, reeling off six diamonds before returning the ♠ 7 for the Rabbit to collect the rest of the tricks.

'Eight down,' gloated H.H. 'I wonder what went wrong. Ha! ha!'

'If you come to think of it,' observed Oscar when we went over the hand later, 'there was nothing much wrong with the bidding or with the lead. The Hog produced an imaginative defence and Papa's deception play was a classic. Everyone, in fact, played well. Only the result was ridiculous.'

'Perhaps,' said P.P., waving a philosophic flipper, 'the Italians are the real villains. Without them, the Rabbit wouldn't have led the two and then the Hog wouldn't have played the knave and then. . . .'

21. Thirteen Wrong Cards

'The irresistible force meets the immovable object,' said Colin the Corgi. 'I wonder which of the two will win.'

Karapet Djoulikyan, the unluckiest player outside outer space, was playing in our monthly duplicate with fortune's favourite, the Rueful Rabbit. On the last set of boards they were due to meet the Hideous Hog and Papa the Greek. It was an unusual combination and there was much speculation among the Griffins as to how it had come into being.

'I agreed to play with him', explained Papa in confidence, 'just to show you all that I can win with anyone, yes, even with him.'

The Hog put it differently. 'People have complained', he said, 'that I never play with weak partners in these events. It isn't true, of course, but just to prove it I've accepted Papa tonight.'

I missed the first of the three boards in the last round, but I heard all about it from Papa while we waited for the results in the bar. These were the East-West hands.

```
        ♠ K J 3                    ♠ 4 2
        ♡ K 7 3          N         ♡ A Q 4 2
        ♢ 9 8        W       E     ♢ A K J 10
        ♣ A K Q 10 5     S         ♣ 8 7 6
```

West	East
Papa	H.H.
1 ♣	1 ♡
2 NT	4 NT
6 NT	

'North leads the ♠ 9. South follows with the ♠ 5 and I win

with the ♠ J. How should I continue?' asked Papa in a threatening voice. It boded ill for anyone who said the wrong thing.

'If the hearts break 3–3, I'm home, so I'll try that first,' said someone. 'If the hearts don't oblige, I'll play South for the ♠ A. After all, he's pretty well marked with it on the lead.'

Oscar the Owl shook his head. 'Too late,' he said. 'South may well have the thirteenth heart as well as the ♠ A, and if so, he'll jump up with the ace and cash his heart. No, you can test the clubs if you like, but you mustn't develop any other suit before going for the ♠ K.'

'Of course,' cried the Greek excitedly, 'I agree absolutely. In fact, there's no problem—unless there's a lunatic at the table, then. . . .'

'But there *was* a lunatic at the table,' broke in the Hog, 'to wit, my partner. Every East-West pair in the room made thirteen tricks, without scoring a single trick in spades. Yet Papa, who was presented with a trick on the lead and had, therefore, fourteen on top, contrived to go three down!'

'Against a mad, crazy, demented lead,' protested Papa, filling in the hands.

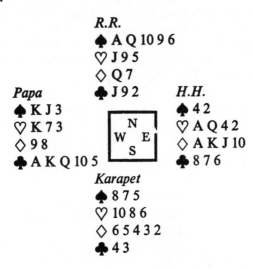

R.R.
♠ A Q 10 9 6
♡ J 9 5
◇ Q 7
♣ J 9 2

Papa
♠ K J 3
♡ K 7 3
◇ 9 8
♣ A K Q 10 5

H.H.
♠ 4 2
♡ A Q 4 2
◇ A K J 10
♣ 8 7 6

Karapet
♠ 8 7 5
♡ 10 8 6
◇ 6 5 4 3 2
♣ 4 3

'As Oscar has just pointed out, I couldn't afford to touch the red suits before taking—er—establishing, that is, my ♠ K. I assumed a sane defence—wrongly as I now know to my cost,' he added bitterly.

'You played against the odds, Papa,' said Karapet with a sigh. 'You should have known that if there was an ace out, no Djouli-kyan was likely to have it. Do you know how many rubbers I have lost since Tuesday? Let me. . . .'

'Ridiculous!' cried a kibitzer. 'Absurd!' echoed another. 'Who has ever heard of leading away from an A Q against a slam?'

With beads of perspiration on his forehead the Rabbit pleaded for mercy. 'What *could* I have led?' he asked piteously. 'I had thirteen wrong cards. Which one should I have chosen?'

After studying the matter closely we agreed that spades, hearts, diamonds and clubs could be ruled out. A lead from the Rabbit's holding in any one of those suits might easily cost a trick, maybe even two tricks.

'Very well then,' observed O.O. broadmindedly, 'perhaps a spade was no worse than anything else. But why pick the nine?'

The Rabbit's brow cleared. 'The fourth highest of my longest suit,' he explained. 'It's in all the books. You multiply by eleven and. . . .'

'Against a slam?' exclaimed Colin the Corgi incredulously, 'but that's senseless.'

'Precisely,' said R.R. nodding vigorously. 'That's just what I thought. Every card I played would be wrong, but the nine of spades would be so much more wrong than any of the others that no one would believe it, so it would be just as if I hadn't done it. Two wrongs often make a right, don't they, and though it cost us a trick, it cost the declarer four, so it did not turn out so badly. I mean. . . .'

Exit—the Ace

The Rabbit was still dithering when I got to the table to watch the last two boards of the evening. For the sake of convenience I make R.R. sit South in the diagram.

Karapet
♠ 4
♡ 3 2
♢ K 5 4 2
♣ A Q 10 6 5 2

```
    ┌─────┐
    │  N  │
    │ W E │
    │  S  │
    └─────┘
```

R.R.
♠ 3 2
♡ A K Q J 10
♢ 7 6
♣ J 9 7

North	South
1 ♣	1 ♡
2 ♣	4 ♡

The Hog opened the ♠ 7 and Papa's king held the first trick.
Winning the heart return, the Rabbit drew trumps, which broke
3–3, and ran the knave of clubs, losing to Papa's king. The Greek,
who could count eleven tricks against him, shrugged his shoulders
and cashed his ♢ A. Then he threw in his hand.

'Saboteur! Quisling!' thundered the Hog. 'Why didn't you take
your ♠ A?'

'Because I didn't have it,' roared back the outraged Greek.

'Nobody seems to have had it,' observed the Armenian
gloomily, looking at the Rabbit's hand. 'A very curious distribution.'

One of the lesser kibitzers, who had been trying to articulate for
some time, managed at last to blurt out several coherent syllables.
'There's a c-card in there,' he said pointing to the board, 'in the
S-south s-s-slot.'

Blushing, the Rabbit hastily retrieved the card which he had left
behind. It was the missing ♠ A.

'Sorry, Karapet,' he said guiltily, 'my carelessness has cost us a trick. Obviously, I needn't have lost that first spade. Everyone else, I suppose, made a trick more. It was all that talk about the last hand.'

'Don't worry, R.R.,' the Armenian spoke with understanding. 'Even when my side is dealt an ace, fate takes it away. It's not your fault. It's the curse of the Djouli. . . .' Karapet's voice trailed off as he studied the travelling score-sheet. 'Amazing,' he murmured. 'Most of them ended up in 4 ♡ and all went down except R.R. . . . without that ace, too.' This was the deal in full.

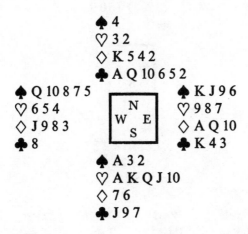

```
                    ♠ 4
                    ♡ 3 2
                    ◇ K 5 4 2
                    ♣ A Q 10 6 5 2
♠ Q 10 8 7 5             ♠ K J 9 6
♡ 6 5 4            N     ♡ 9 8 7
◇ J 9 8 3      W     E   ◇ A Q 10
♣ 8                S    ♣ K 4 3
                    ♠ A 3 2
                    ♡ A K Q J 10
                    ◇ 7 6
                    ♣ J 9 7
```

Pointing Papa's cigar like a gun at the Armenian, the Hog addressed him in a solemn voice. 'I suppose you realize, Karapet, that if declarer discovers prematurely that he has the ♠ A, he cannot make the contract. Follow the play. The ♠ A wins the first trick. A second spade is ruffed, but not the third for there's no way back to the closed hand without using dummy's last trump. When the club finesse fails, East gives me, West, the lead with a spade and I play a diamond through dummy's king. Neither can declarer clear clubs before drawing trumps for I would then ruff the second club. No, by far the best way to make the contract is to bury the ace of spades in the South slot before trick one. It needs perfect timing though.'

'No need to jeer,' retorted the Rabbit with quiet dignity. 'I didn't do it on purpose. You ought to know that.'

Approach Bidding

On the last board of the evening, North-South were vulnerable
and the Rabbit, sitting South, dealt.

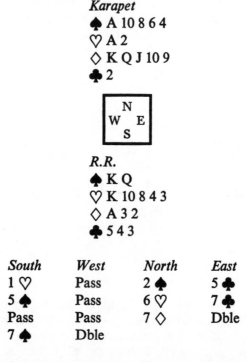

Karapet
♠ A 10 8 6 4
♡ A 2
◇ K Q J 10 9
♣ 2

R.R.
♠ K Q
♡ K 10 8 4 3
◇ A 3 2
♣ 5 4 3

South	West	North	East
1 ♡	Pass	2 ♠	5 ♣
5 ♠	Pass	6 ♡	7 ♣
Pass	Pass	7 ◇	Dble
7 ♠	Dble		

Karapet's jump to 2 ♠ had its critics, though all agreed that his
hand was not easy to describe. But it was the Rabbit whose predica-
ment evoked most sympathy. Who could blame him for squirming
over Papa's leap into 5 ♣? Of course he could pass. Yet surely the
king and queen of the suit in which partner forces must be worth
something. Besides, there's such a thing as *amour propre*. One
doesn't like to be shouted down—not by Papa, anyway, In a firm
voice the Rabbit bid 5 ♠. The Hog passed, looking a shade too
bored, I thought, and the Armenian shut his eyes in search of
inspiration. With a singleton club he felt sure that there was a

slam about. But what in? Sensing the problem which the Greek's pre-emptive bid might have posed for the Rabbit, Karapet tried 6 ♡. It was a master bid, he told us later, which allowed partner to choose the trump suit without carrying any suggestion of a grand slam. To this day Papa maintains that his imaginative bid of 7 ♣ was an example of perfect psychology. He had taken opponents completely out of their stride. Neither knew what the other was doing and since there was every hope of a tragic mis-understanding, it followed that the stage for it should be set at the highest level.

The Rabbit, fearing that he had said too much already, passed gratefully and Karapet once more closed his eyes to seek inspiration. It came to him in a flash. Clearly the Rabbit had made a forcing pass. Therefore he had no club loser and the grand slam was a certainty—so long as he chose the right trump suit. Hence 7 ♢, an approach bid prepared for every response.

Papa doubled on principle and the Hog drew a deep breath the better to deal with 7 ♠. A glance at his hand will help to understand his feelings.

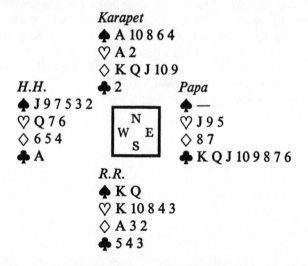

Karapet
♠ A 10 8 6 4
♡ A 2
♢ K Q J 10 9
♣ 2

H.H.
♠ J 9 7 5 3 2
♡ Q 7 6
♢ 6 5 4
♣ A

Papa
♠ —
♡ J 9 5
♢ 8 7
♣ K Q J 10 9 8 7 6

R.R.
♠ K Q
♡ K 10 8 4 3
♢ A 3 2
♣ 5 4 3

Toying with a gold-tipped cigarette in either hand, Papa thought deeply. Had the Hog made a Lightner double? It was quite likely and, if so, a heart lead was clearly indicated. Anyway it was safe, while there was nothing to gain by leading a club. After all, opponents wouldn't have called a grand slam with a quick loser in the suit called against them.

As the ♡ 5 touched the green baize and dummy went down, the Armenian's black eyebrows rose an inch or so. For a moment the customary expression of melancholy gave way to one of bewilderment. He had expected confidently at least one more spade, not to mention a reputable heart or two in place of the midgets. As for the three baby clubs, he couldn't think where they sprang from. Of course, he reflected philosophically, he should have known that things were not what they seemed when he picked up the best hand seen by a Djoulikyan for two generations at least.

A good loser, through constant practice, Karapet was ready to go down fighting.

Dummy's eight, the Hog's queen and Karapet's ace made up the first trick. The heart finesse allowed the Armenian to discard his ♣ 2 on the ♡ K. A club ruff was followed by three rounds of diamonds ending on the table and with trumps only left H.H. was compelled to ruff dummy's next lead, the ♣ 3. Karapet over-ruffed in the closed hand and trumped a diamond with the ♠ K. Now a heart was ruffed and overruffed and declarer's last diamond was trumped with the ♠ Q. Sitting with the ♠ A 10 over the Hog's J 9, and with the lead in dummy, the Armenian made the last two tricks. Twice the Hog had been compelled to underruff. Four times he had been overruffed.

'What on earth did you double on?' cried Papa indignantly.